The Eager Soldier

An Australian journalist's account of his life and the Great War

Compiled by Laurel Kathleen McIntyre and Barbara Adams

Edited by Heather Eaton

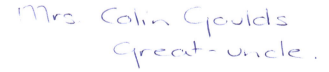

Mrs. Colin Goulds
Great-uncle.

Inquiries should be made to:
Seaview Press
PO Box 7339
West Lakes, South Australia 5021
Telephone 08 8242 0666; fax 08 8242 0333
E-mail: seaview@seaviewpress.com.au
Web site: http://www.seaviewpress.com.au

Printed by:
Salmat Document Management Solutions Pty Limited
11 East Terrace, Mile End, South Australia 5031.

National Library of Australia Cataloguing-in-Publication entry
  Wright, Theodore Willard, 1893- .
  The eager soldier : an Australian journalist's account of his life
  and the Great War.

  ISBN 9781740084222.
  1. Wright, Theodore Willard, 1893- - Diaries. 2. Australia.
  Army. Australian Imperial Force (1914-1921). 3. Journalists
  - Australia - Biography. 4. World War, 1914-1918 - Biography.
  I. McIntyre, Laurel Kathleen, 1903- . II. Adams, Barbara Rae,
  1931- . III. Eaton, Heather Joy, 1962- . IV. Title.

  940.3092

Theodore Willard Wright

No. 937

43rd Battalion A.I.F.

(Machine Gun Section)

Born: 30th December 1892

This book is dedicated to
'Young Un'
Laurel Kathleen McIntyre (nee Wright),
whose love of family history made
this book possible

Foreword

Theodore Willard Wright was born in Mount Gambier South Australia on 30th December 1892 and died on July 31st 1917 aged 25 years and seven months in the battle of Messines at Warneton in Belgium. At his memorial service his age was stated as 24 years and seven months, but this is incorrect according to the copy that I have of his birth registration.

One of my earliest memories is of my mother speaking of her brother Theo, who died in the First World War. His photographs adorned our home and he looked so handsome in his uniform. Moved by the tragedy of it all, I hung on her every word and he became a romantic figure in my imagination.

Theo was a lad of ten when my mother was born. He dearly loved this youngest sister, the baby of the family, and she adored him in return. At the time of his enlistment he was aged twenty-three and she was thirteen. He was never far from her thoughts, and frequent were the anecdotes related in the family about the great times that the siblings had enjoyed together. In the ensuing years after his death, my mother souvenired, from her mother and other family members, all the letters and other memorabilia pertaining to my uncle that she possibly could. Hence this book became a possibility.

Theo began his working life with his father who was a builder. As it was apparent that he had an impressive talent for the written word he was encouraged to become a journalist. The most likely way to achieve that goal in those days was to work one's way up through the system by becoming employed at a newspaper in any capacity. This is the path that he chose. Theo appears to have begun his career working for the Mount Gambier *Star*. He then tried his hand at retail, by the opening of a shop at Oakbank, before returning to the joint vocation of journalist/monoline operator at the Petersburg (later the name was changed to Peterborough[1]) *Mercury* newspaper, and again at the *Star*, where he was employed at the time of his enlistment. Nowadays he would be described as multi-skilled.

Nevertheless Theo left no stone unturned to go to the War and he eventually left Australia with a willing heart. What an adventure it must have seemed for a young man, who, but for the advent of the World War, could never have aspired to travel overseas and broaden his horizon.

I read his letters as a girl, but it was only in my later years that I had the time to explore the possibility of them being published. It is such a pity that records such as these are a 'dying thing' as email, mobile phones and SMS messaging have taken over our society. His letters tell so much about his character and the lifestyle of those times before the motor car, where travel was by either train, horse back or horse and buggy.

Theo's letters begin with his first employment away from home in 1913, his subsequent many attempts to enlist after the outbreak of war, the several refusals due to his false teeth, and the eventual dispensing by the authorities with that ban, as more and more 'cannon fodder' was needed for the war. (Before being enlisted he was required to eat a Bush Biscuit in front of the recruiting officer.) His journalistic flair is apparent throughout his correspondence, and his deep love of his family shines through.

A few letters to his cousins have survived and in those he was more explicit about the actions in which he was involved. He would not have wanted to worry his mother with such information.

One must keep in mind that photocopying was non-existent, and so the letters were passed around the family, from member

---

1 The *Sydney Morning Herald* states: "The change of the town's name occurred in 1917 when anti-German sentiment was so strong that the *Nomenclature Act* insisted that all German-sounding names be changed. It then became Peterborough and never changed back." (17th February 2005)

to member. Notations were made on the pages as this process occurred, but these have been omitted.

Sadly Theo's correspondence with his unofficial fiancée, Ivey Opie, was lost. It was not considered the right thing to do to propose to a girl before you were in a financial position to support a wife and family; most certainly not when you were going off to a war. However in one of his early letters he confides in his mother that, "Ivey is the one for me". She did not marry for many years after his death and at the age of 33 died in childbirth along with her infant. Had Theo lived that tragedy would quite possibly have been his to endure. In such vagaries lies the hand of fate!

Theo had five sisters. These were Bertha (Bert), Constance (Connie), Daisy, Millicent (Millie) and Laurel (Laurie). There also was one brother, Fred. Daisy and Millie both married farmers and lived well into their nineties. Bertha married Ron Osman, who rose through the 'Railways' to the position of Stationmaster at the Adelaide Railway Station. Constance married George Hicks, and moved to Victoria, where her descendants now live. Fred became a Postmaster, a position of some standing in those times.

Laurel, my mother, married a baker, James (Jim) McIntyre. She is occasionally referred to in his letters as the 'Little un' or 'Young un'. The references to Aunt Jane are explained by the fact that Theo's mother Alice, one of seventeen children, was given away to her Aunt Jane and Uncle William at the age of six. It was considered selfish to not do so when one had so many children and a sister who was childless. Aunt Jane then became Alice's adopted mother, and as such was cared for in her old age by her 'daughter'.

Theo's efforts to get his teeth fixed are related in his letters, first by saving up for his false teeth, then his losing them on a swimming trip, necessitating the saving up yet again for a second set! Unfortunately he lost the second pair as well. The desire to be part of the conflict and thereby not being seen as a coward, were dominant characteristics of those times. Men who were not in uniform were often looked down on, and many were presented with white feathers, a symbol of cowardice. I have reprinted in its actual form the correspondence Theo had with the war office, and the one letter in particular, which he wrote on the eve of his death, in his own handwriting. That letter moved me to tears.

Patriotism was a strong influence, as becomes apparent in his letters. Allegiance to King and Country were also very motivating factors. In the year 2000 and again in the year 2004 my partner, Barry Allison, and I visited the Flanders Fields and it was then that I discovered for the first time that Theo's body was never found, although his name is faithfully inscribed on the Menin Gate. We saw actual newsreels of those fields with trenches two metres deep in mud. For the first time we were able to realise why so many bodies were lost as they sank into this quagmire. An allied soldier died every 19 seconds in those Fields. They ran red with blood, as the seasonal poppies bloomed also in red, hence the wearing of a red poppy on November the eleventh (the anniversary of the first World War Armistice).

I understand from correspondence from Theo's fellow soldiers that he was buried near a Windmill. We sought to find the exact place, but due to language barriers were unable to discover it; the Windmill had been long ago demolished.

I am grateful for the editing of the letters by my niece Heather Eaton, who is an author in her own right. Thank you also to Mary Shadbolt for typing most of the manuscript.

Barbara Adams

Contents

Foreword...v

1913–1915...1

1916..45

1917..145

Aftermath...215

1913-1915

Oakbank
Thursday 15/5/13

Dear Father,

Although I have not yet received that letter from you, I intend to write you again and try to give you an account of further developments. This place seems to have a beneficial effect on us all. Speaking for myself – well, I haven't felt so well for a long time – have a tremendous appetite, can sleep well, and feel generally pretty fit. That, I think, describes the situation with the lot of us.

I have to smile when I think of the plans we made before leaving home; how we thought we would be at it straightaway, and I thought it would be necessary to secure a horse even before going to town. As things have turned out, there is little likelihood of the shop being opened this week.[2]

'Winch' would not let the men inside to effect renovations, so they were only able to start on the exterior of the premises, and the result of their work is satisfactory. The place had to be practically re-roofed, as the rain was getting in nearly everywhere. The man who is now working at the place is a brother-in-law of our landlord (Mr. Obsorne), and he said this morning that Osborne had already spent about eighty pounds on the place.

In order that work could be proceeded with, all the stock had to be taken from the shelves and other fixings; and, by Jove, I can assure you, things were in a terrible state; the stock was dusty and the shelves absolutely covered with dust. When the things were removed, the walls were repaired and calcimined. To-day the ceiling of the shop has been cleaned

---

2 Theo grew up in Mount Gambier and began his working life there. In 1913 he moved to Oakbank to open a General Store.

and varnishing of same nearly finished. I have been hard at work helping the man; we will be able to get in sooner as a result of my assistance.

Half of each window has been 'frosted', and to-morrow I am going to clean them, and I expect the job will take some time, for they are pretty dirty. The carpenter will also be at work enlarging and glazing the two small windows; and putting two fresh panes of glass and making a suitable window, one of which is boarded up at present.

This afternoon Mr. Osborne came on a visit of inspection. (I went to him on Tuesday and had a bit of a talk and he promised to come out today and have a look at things.)

He _did_ get a shock. He said he had no idea that the place was in such a shocking state; had he known it was so bad he said he would not have touched it. He is a jolly good fellow and everything we asked him to do he said he would have it done. The place is to be thoroughly repaired, and I'm afraid it will be quite a month before we can occupy the living rooms.

The place is to be painted, some rooms papered, others calcimined, a new mantelpiece in every room with the exception of one which has a nice one in it now, a new window or two, and sundry other matters are to receive attention.

Our every request was granted. 'Well,' said Mr. Osborne, 'I can't do anything else but agree, for it's absolutely necessary.'

I suppose it will be a week or two before you and Millie arrive, and by that time things ought to be improving. Really, you won't be able to realise the state the place is in and what we have been 'up against'. I can see 'heaps' of work ahead, but I'm not sorry; so far I am pretty well satisfied, and I have hopes that the venture will turn out alright.

It's no good trying to do 'biz' with things as they are, and we are convinced that we will create a much better impression by getting everything in 'apple-pie' order before making a bid for the custom of the 'Oakbankites'.

In the meantime I think the Wright family are creating a favorable impression, and everyone seems to look with approval on the repairs and improvements which are now being effected.

Of course we don't know what prices to charge for things, but hope to get the 'run' of it before we open up. I wrote to Con asking if she could secure one of *Charlick*'s price-lists. We have one from *Wilkinson*'s, but it is rather baffling. Anyway we will get on alright. My mind is very much easier now that the landlord has agreed to have things brought 'up to the knocker'.

I suppose you know that I am staying at Edwards'. They are farmers and have a medium-sized horse for sale. The price wanted is only eight pounds. It is young – 3 years – I had a ride on it the other night and it went alright. I don't know whether the horse is a mare or gelding. As the price is low, I am inclined to think there must be something wrong. One of their horses was injured yesterday (a hay-knife cut it) so they are now working the chestnut, and there may not be an opportunity just now for me to give it a trial in harness. I haven't forgotten how to handle a horse!

I hope that things are well with you; and also that our home here will be in good order, and a business footing fairly established by the time you arrive.

With love from us all,
Your loving son,
"Theo"

… Please, mother dear, let me know your financial position. Father said he would let me know when he required help from me, but never refers to the matter.

A man came to me in trouble yesterday. Some time ago he backed a bill for a mate, for twenty-five pounds. That mate cleared out after the first payment and left the other fellow to pay his bill. This chap had paid all except the last installment, which he sent away on Thursday. That left him very short, and as his wife is in a very delicate state of health he did not wish to worry her over the matter, and as the kiddies wanted things and his wife wondered why he didn't get them, he did not know what to do. He is a member of our church and knows me, for I play tennis with Walkers' next door to where he lives. I lent him five pounds, and an order to collect his pay on Thursday week secures me from loss.

You know, mother, I can picture father as he was the first night he came to Oakbank, standing there and saying, 'Well, I'm here to finance the scheme'. Then came his totally different conduct later. Now he has built the Evandale home. When I came to town to see about joining the first contingent, and on the way to the station with me on my return, he said when I asked him, that it was alright, that he still had something to fall back on. I would like to know just how you stand.

Poor mother, dear, I wonder when things are to become easier for you. I do wish my luck would change, then things would be easier. Do you know members of the expeditionary forces receive 35/- (thirty-five shillings) a week besides their keep?

An epidemic of ptomaine poisoning has struck the town, resulting from ice-cream served at one of the refreshment shops. Lionel Fletcher lectured here on Thursday regarding the early closing question and afterwards a great number went to this place opposite the town hall for refreshments. As a result all those having ice-cream are seriously ill, some more so than others, but all have the trouble in a particularly distressful form. One death, that of a boy of 12, has occurred, while one or two other cases it's feared will result in a like manner.

I had a particularly hard day on Thursday, not having finished till 3 a.m. Friday. At about 10 p.m. I went out to the front for a breather, (for the weather has been terribly hot) and thought of having some refreshment at this shop which is very near our works, but ultimately I decided not to. My 'guardian angel' must have been watching o'er me alright then, don't you think so?

You will see by the paper what I did on the holiday. I couldn't play tennis for 'nuts' and got a big hiding in the singles, 6-1. My racquet is cracked, and I'll never play so well again till I can afford a new one, which, at this rate, will never be.

Work is very slack and the foreman has been off for the whole of this week. I wish things would liven up a bit.

We have been experiencing vile weather – terrible heat and awful dust storms, but as my health this summer is excellent I have stood the conditions well. I do wish that you, father and Laurie were as well as I, but I do hope that things will improve.

What do you think, mother dear, 'Tiny' Gerlach, my giant school teacher friend paid me a compliment the other day, and coming from 'Tiny', who is a very sarcastic brute, I treasured it the more. I remarked, 'Jove, Tiny, you do make me feel a weed'. Then he said 'Don't you worry. Ted, I consider you are very well put together'. Others of my pals have remarked favourably on my strength and fitness, for which I am glad.

One of these school teacher pals of mine, Jack Nicholls, who is slightly my senior, stays with a newly married couple, Mr. and Mrs. Will Day, next door, and I am often in there. Will is a railway fitter and rather big and strong. He and Jack were having a bit of a rough-and-tumble, so I afterwards had a 'go' at Will and more than held my own. We shifted the table and fell to. I scored two falls in my favor to his one, when he had enough. So you see I'm not too bad physically.

Well, I think I will close now, with the hope that your health may improve, and that other uninviting prospects may be either removed or subdued.

With fondest love to all, and especially your own dear self,
Yours lovingly,
"Theo"

Copy of Testimonial
From *South-Eastern Star* Printing & Publishing Company
Mt. Gambier.

September 13th, 1913

This is to certify that Mr. Theo Wright was in my employ for 5 years, during which time he held the position of monoline operator. He proved himself to be a good all-round man, having a knowledge of jobbing, etc., besides the monoline work. He is of a temperate life and worthy of all confidence. Of his ability I have formed a very high opinion and have no hesitation in commending him to anybody that may be wishful of securing the services of a capable and reliable man.

(signed) Alf, Clarke
Proprietor
South-Eastern Star Printing & Publishing Company

6 a.m.[3]

Dear Home Folks,

I'm sorry that I did not get my letter to you written on Sunday. The fact is I was out riding on horseback in the morning, driving in the afternoon 'til late, and then went to church at night, which made rather a full program.

As I believe I told you, they intended coming; the Southwark Basketball team played us on Saturday night in the gymnasium here. I was included in the home team. It was terribly hot playing and the game was very fast and even.

Most of us had pretty sore bodies next day from coming in contact with the floor, and our opponents, but such things as that are only a mere detail. We came off victorious in the end, but just managed it, for the scores were Petersburg 18 goals, Southwark 16 goals.

At the conclusion of the match the members of the Ladies' Physical Culture Club provided a lovely spread, in the Methodist schoolroom. There was speechifying and general high jinks. (They made me attempt to propose the toast of 'The Ladies'!) The girls waited on the boys, so while they were having their refreshments three of us *Times* chaps did the washing up. I got into a row for breaking a tumbler, and one of the ladies (we call her Mum) said she'd kiss me if I didn't behave myself. Altogether we had a tip-top time.

I have made numerous good friends of both sexes here, included are three sons of the German parson (Rev. Hass); it was through them that I had such a good time on Sunday. They intended taking Mr. Leicester and I for a drive at 10a.m.; we

3 This letter was written some time in 1913. Theo Willard Wright had left his former employment with the Mount Gambier South-Eastern Star Printing & Publishing Company. After that he moved to Oakbank but his venture there seemed short lived. Later he moved to Petersburg (later called Peterborough) to work for the *Quorn Mercury* Newspaper.

did not wake up till 10 minutes to 10, and even when I did get round there the Hass brothers (and sister) were just going to have breakfast.

After breakfast we groomed the horses well and were fooling round generally, so Miss Hass said we ought to wait till the afternoon and then go for a drive. We decided to do so. Walter Hass said he and I would go for a bit of a ride and see if we could get a conveyance large enough to take the Southwark chaps (8) with us after dinner. So off we went.

The horses we rode were lovely greys, especially the one I was astride, and you bet your life I was as pleased as Punch. By Jove, she is a beauty, and can trot like fury and is showy too. So you can picture us sailing through the main street as the people were returning from church. We got a light trolley, fitted with seats, for the afternoon's excursion.

After dinner I went round to Hass's again and we got the horses ready and started off. We hadn't been able to let the fellows know what we intended doing, but we had to chance picking them up. We were lucky to find them all banded together in the main street with some of our own chaps, so we took 'em all aboard, sixteen of us altogether, with only two light little horses. But by Jove, they did travel even with such a load as that. We had intended to go through Yongala[4] to some creek or other, but had pity on the ponies and did not go any further than Yongala. We had a bonza[5] outing, the visitors were nice chaps, and we did not get home till about 6 o'clock, so we had to bustle some to get to church.

Last night the carriage and pair, with Wally Hass and Hardy Leicester (my room mate) on board, called round here at the *Times* to take me for a spin, but I could not get away.

---

4 A nearby small town.

5 BONZA: *noun* something which excites admiration by being outstandingly good of its kind.

On Wednesday last I had just about the time of my life. Our gymnasium clique of young ladies and chaps went to the Jamestown Show, leaving here at 10.20 a.m., and taking provisions to make a picnic of it. By the way the young ladies and chaps here are absolutely the most sociable crowd I've ever met (that is, the members of the Gymnasium here, I've not met many others yet). They made me feel at home at once and I'm a good pal with them, one and all.

Although I've been working day and night since I came here, I am also having a very good time on the occasions when I happen to get away from the machines for a time. The lady I referred to, as 'Mum', is mother to all the young folk here. Although she's about forty she doesn't look anywhere near that age. Miss Leak (that's her name), can play tennis, basketball, or any sport for that matter, with the best, and she looks after all our crowd and everyone of us call her 'Mum'.

She's a dear old sport.

To get back to Wednesday's outing. We journeyed down in the trucks, but it was much cooler than in the carriages, and we stirred things up a bit. Arrived at Jamestown about 12.30 or so, and my word, I did get a surprise for 'tis quite a pretty place and a good size. I expected to see a dry, treeless spot like Petersburg[6].

When 'Mum' had got her 'chicks' together we had dinner. There were about 20 in our party, so you can imagine the time we had. While we were having dessert I leaned back for some reason or other and got my back covered with apricot and cream; had my coat off, which was just as well.

The show itself and the inside exhibition were very good. While one young lady and I were wandering round in the

---

6 The town of Petersburg was renamed (along with around 70 other South Australian towns with German names) Peterborough in 1917, due to the conflict of the first World War.

afternoon most of the others were taken for a spin in a motor, so at tea time we were bewailing the fact that we, with a couple of other girls, had missed it. So the owner of the car, who was with our party while at the show, said we should have a ride, and after tea took us for a spin. We started at 7 o'clock, when it was lovely and cool, and did not get back till 8, with there being in the car three girls, the driver and myself. Needless to say we had a bonnie time. We didn't leave Jamestown for Petersburg 'til 9.30 p.m., and had a gay time coming home (eh, what!). It was midnight before I turned in.

Petersburg
Sept. 22nd 1913

Dear Home Folks
Here I am a day late with my correspondence, but I hope it will not be less acceptable because of that. I was working yesterday, and was thus prevented from writing. However, I hope this will be the first and last time that your letter will not get away by Monday morning's express. I plead extenuating circumstances as my excuse for working yesterday because what I did was very needful and as a result I have had a better time this morning.

Unfortunately, however, I did not get the *Quorn Mercury*[7] set up in time to catch the train, and I s'pose I'll find Daddy Bennett way up the pole when I get back!! My happy troubles, though. It was my own fault partly, and partly the fault of the folks here, for they didn't call me early enough nor have breakfast ready as early as I could wish, so that the metal in my machine was not melted as soon as it should have been. But

_____

7 Theo worked as a monoline operator producing the *Quorn Mercury* newspaper.

in the past when I have asked them a couple of times to have breakfast ready and then to call me, I have taken my time in turning out. So I suppose it serves me right.

Mr. Romey asked me round to tea last night but I begged to be excused, so I may go when I like.

What do you think? Mr Clark wrote last week, forwarding me a bonza reference and also offering me my old billet at 25/- a week, with improved conditions!!! Had it been anywhere else but The Mount I might have snapped it. But as Mr. Bennett kept this job open for me for a fortnight, and as things are now fast improving I intend to remain on here. Clark wanted me to let him know my decision as soon as possible, but I haven't wired him yet. I intend doing so when I return to work in a few minutes time.

I received a private wire from Roper Hill at dinnertime, advising me to reply at once if I wanted the position. I'd like to go back, and yet I'd rather stay here and have decided on the latter course for better or worse.

Later

Have wired Clark that I can't go; so there's another matter disposed of.

Well, last week has been an equally trying one, but there's every promise of a better result this week. The American boys will be here on Thursday, and I have reserved seats for a friend and myself along with another chap from the office who has the two seats alongside. We are looking forward to a good time. So I'm trying my level best to get enough up to fix the paper before tea time Thursday, for it will be a go, if I am prevented from going.

The boss wasn't at all cross because the *Mercury* was too late for the train.

Two of the young chaps at the office are great gymnasium

enthusiasts, and I have caught the fever now and hope soon to be able to keep my end up among the boys there. Basketball is the favourite sport, and they have teams of girls, little boys and big boys. The latter team made a trip to town about a fortnight ago, but were beaten. The girls' team are going to have a try in about a fortnight's time. They are not too bad at the game either.

The Methodists had a bazaar here on Saturday, and it was very successful for they took about sixty-seven pounds. Not bad, eh, for an afternoon and evening! I went, and had a fair time, but you know what stale old things bazaars are.

I had a talk to the boss, while I was at the office yesterday, re my compensation. I will continue at piecework, but he will guarantee me two pounds a week. I ought soon to be able to make anything between that sum and three pounds. Anyway, I'm going to have a good try. If I have a bad run any time, I will be sure of my two pounds, if no more.

With regard to the parcel, which I understand was forwarded to me about a week or more ago, I have been to the station several times about it but there's no sign of it yet; neither has the invoice come through. So I am wondering where the goods can have got too. Another thing. The return fare from here to town is twenty-five shillings. Mr. Kilmeyer charged me twenty-seven shillings and sixpence single from Balhannah to Petersburg; so I reckon he made a mistake and charged me double fare from town here. I thought when he told me the fare that it seemed rather stiff.

I haven't had any opportunity for indulging in any tennis, so far, but hope now to be able to get some play in. Took my racket down to have a couple of strings in tonight, but it won't be ready 'til Thursday.

You all tell me not to do so much night work but you know, beggars can't be choosers. I hope things will look up henceforth.

Many thanks for letters received. It must be lively at the dances now, with so few boys present. I wish I could go for a walk to Fern Gully, girls.

I'm sorry that mother and Laurie[8] were hurt because their names were not mentioned in my last epistle, but you know, dears, you are all included. I hope you are all well – Mother, Father, Daisy, Millie and Laurie! And I hope that business is improving now that the season has improved. We have had a little rain lately, but a great deal is needed to do the required amount of good.

Dear Mother, I am greatly distressed that I forgot to recognise your birthday. I was keeping it in mind, and had not altogether forgotten it; if you only knew or could realise what I have been through since my arrival here, you would, I know, willingly forgive me. I hope the card I am sending, although only an insignificant little thing, will convey to you all the love and good wishes that I extend to you.

I must close now, dear ones, and start on a report of the bazaar[9], so *Au Revoir* for another week!

Yours lovingly,
"Theo"

Petersburg
Feb. 15th, 1914

Dear All,

This is the first letter that you will receive from me, that has been written in my new diggings. I have just had my first meal here. I was supposed to come to this place for tea last evening

---

8 Laurel Kathleen Wright – Theo's youngest sibling.

9 Theo also wrote articles for the *Quorn Mercury*

but went to Hass's instead. Five of us went for a drive about 9.30 or so, and about 11 o'clock picked up another passenger (Miss Paula Hass) and even then we did not go home, but continued driving for some little time longer.

I won't tell you what time we did get home in case you may be shocked, but we were not driving all the time. Anyway, Miss Hass said it was too late for me to come home, as my new landlady would think I was an awful stop-out. So they made up a bed for me on the veranda. I was preparing to leave to come here for breakfast this morning, but they wouldn't allow me to come, and, I didn't arrive here until dinnertime.

Last night while driving we had rather a narrow escape from a nasty accident. We were nearing a crossing and could not hear the alarm bell, which was ringing, with the result that we were only a few feet from the line when a long train flashed over the crossing. Young Hass had hold of the ribbons but the horses were hard to haul up so his sister, who was nearest, grabbed the reins, while I jumped out and caught them by the heads, and we managed to keep 'em standing some feet clear. However it was a nasty fright.

The crossing is a horrible one as it is impossible to see if a train is coming and to hear either the train or the warning bell, owing to the noise of the moving vehicle. So we were almost on to it before we had any idea that a train was in the vicinity. The horses, which I have often told you are a valuable and high-spirited pair, had just been frightened by a drunk when turning towards the crossing, and so were going some. We were lucky, indeed, to escape mishap. As I was stronger than young Hass and the girls seemed to have more confidence in me, I took the reins after that occurrence. The horses were so fit, though, that soon after, when turning a corner they swung the phaeton round on two wheels. Altogether we had an exciting and enjoyable ride.

I have been to Hass's just about every evening this week; there are three girls and three boys. Miss Hass is about 22 or 23, and the others come within about twelve months of each other. They are just alright. I have always been very good friends with them, but more than ever of late. Their mother has been dead many years and Miss Hass has had to take her place; she's a bonza young lady and so are her sisters and brothers.

Their father, the German parson, is to be re-married shortly; the girls are therefore leaving home for Adelaide. Miss Paula leaves by tomorrow morning's express, and Nelda and Theodora are to go in about a fortnight. I'm jolly sorry they're going; I wish I could introduce them to you, as I'm sure you would like them immensely. I'll be rather lonely when they go. I think, though, that the boys will be under the rule of the new mistress. They all wanted me to go to Yongala for a drive this afternoon, but I decided not to. I often go round there for a singsong; half a dozen of us get around the piano and make merry 'til further orders, singing all kinds of songs.

I've had a better time this week with my machine; on Thursday it went beautifully, but then the piston in the engine smashed and thus kept us all night. We haven't any luck at all.

I did not work yesterday afternoon, and when I went for the mail found a lot of correspondence from Quorn. I'm going down this evening to see when I'll have to start; it might mean night work again, but I hope not.

Received your letters yesterday Mother and Millie, and I was very pleased to hear the news. You have had a lovely time, Mother, house and land hunting, and I hope the result will prove satisfactory in the end. Are you going to stay home? Will you like it better, Dais? I hope you are feeling alright now-a-days, old girl. You did not say how you like it at the *Town & Country Stores*, Mill; wouldn't you like it better to be back at John Martin's?

I'm very sorry indeed, Dad, to hear that you are not too well; but hope that you will soon be A1 again.

I guess you are all glad that you are to live near Con's. Won't you be glad to live near Mavis, Laurie? Did you like the card, dear?

I was thinking seriously of taking a run down to town shortly, but that is now impossible. I had three sovs[10] in an envelope in my pocket book and when I went to my bag on Friday, the pocket book was there alright but – empty! Can't think what I have done with the money; I'm a bit absent minded of late, and as 'tis about a fortnight since I went to the pocket book, I've no idea where it is. So there you are – I'm dog poor again, with I.C.S. instalments to keep up, and money wanted for other things. I don't seem to have any luck whatsoever; it makes a chap feel like not troubling a continental what happens. I wanted very much to run down there to see Bert and now that is impossible. I'll have to be mighty tight or I won't be able to afford it at Easter either.

That's about all this time, so *Au Revoir.*
Yours Lovingly,
"Theo"

Dear Young Un
By Jove, Laurie, I can quite sympathise with you, for I have had a bonza cold for about the last three weeks – ever since we played basketball at Terowie – and am only just getting rid of

---

10 Sovereign – a gold coin worth one English pound.

it. I have felt right off colour at times, what with the nasty cold and the long hours at work, but that's only a mere detail. There won't be so much work in hand in future now that the shows are over, which will be quite a relief.

The description of the hills, which you gave mother, was splendid, and made me feel quite Oakbank sick. The hills must be simply glorious now. It's a nice day here today and I'd give a lot to be able to take a walk to Fern Gully, eh what? But I'm going to be good; it's the Baptist Sunday School anniversary and I'm going there to see what kind of a showing they can make.

On Wednesday I went to the local show; had a member's ticket given me by Mr. Bennett, so it did not cost me as much as it would otherwise have done. Went to see a snake side-show and I was handling one and put it round my neck; as it was a carpet snake and harmless there was nothing to fear. Others were poisonous, and to show that such was the case, the owners let them kill some birds. The Showman was putting the snake's heads into his mouth!!!

Have you read of Madame Lena Cossly, the great soprano? Well, she, with her party, is to visit Petersburg on Friday next. I have a ticket entitling *The Times* reporter to <u>two</u> seats, which I'll get reserved tomorrow. As I've not had an opportunity of hearing a great singer, I am looking forward to next Friday's concert.

As things don't seem too good up there, you might be better off if you left. Although I fail to see what you will all do if you were to leave the shop. I hope the gent who is to inspect shortly will come to your terms. I am anxiously awaiting news.

I was sorry to hear that Gert. B. had injured her foot; as I have not had any word from Union Street since leaving Quorn, I was unaware that anything had happened to her. We are still good friends, but I think that is all we will ever be, somehow; this is confidential mind.

I was so glad, dears, to receive those lovely flowers; they were a real taste of home. Are some of them the fruits of the roots which I planted just before I left? I wished they would last longer though. Please send some as often as you like, for they are very scarce here.

That is all for this time, so *Au Revoir.*
With much love to Father, Mother, Daisy, Millie and Laurie, from
"Theo"

Petersburg
Oct. 26th, 1914

Dear All,
I was very pleased indeed to receive the budget from you on Saturday, but was indeed sorry that the news contained therein was not of a happier note. I'll have to add the usual that there's no news to send.

I'm sorry to hear that you are out of work again Dad, and that you, Mother dear, are far from well. Don't work too hard, Mother dear. You must neither work out nor rust out; you know we want to keep you with us for many, many years yet. Perhaps our star will be in the ascendant some day soon, and you will have a happier time. There ought to be a chance for me in town when things straighten out a bit. I hope some of the lino[11] men have volunteered for the front, although that is rather a mean wish, is it not? But, all's fair in love and war,

---

11 Monoline operators

so they say. I haven't heard from either Bert or Daisy since writing them; I owe Fred a letter and will write him one of these days.

It has been very hot again after the rain, and it seems as if the last downpour emptied the heavens, for the skies have been brazen since. Now that the ground has dried up again there is plenty of dust about, but one good thing is that our supplies of water have been replenished and we are able to have a wash now and again.

Owing to the scarcity of paper we are forced to cut down the size of our papers; perhaps I'll have a still easier time then. But I won't work for less than two pounds – I'd sooner go to the front. But I don't think there's any chance of our wages being further curtailed. How are you off for paper, etc Millie?

I received your card alright Mill, and many thanks.

It must have been good fun at the carnival. I'm glad you went to the carnival and I saw by the illustrations in the *Weekly* that it must have been a great turnout.

I went to church last night and it was terribly hot. I was using my hat for a fan all the time; I did not care so long as I was kept cool. Afterwards a boy pal and I went for a stroll and it was quite lovely after the close atmosphere in church. One thing about this place is that the evenings outside are cool and it is always a refresher to take a stroll after tea. I've changed my habits abso-(bally)-lutely. I'm generally in bed between 9 and 10 and up about 6, and so am pretty fit. I'm able to do a bit of drawing again now.

This is not altogether a (blanky) desert. In one or two homes where the owners have a windmill, the gardens are just beautiful. There is a garden about a couple of hundred yards from here which is simply a paradise and looks more like a suburban home, as it would have looked in favourable times – not as they are now. It does one good to come into contact with such beauty in such arid surroundings. But the soil here, when well watered, will grow anything, so they say. And such cases as the above quite bear out those statements. If you have a try at the contracting, Dad, I hope that you will have every success, and in any case I hope things will be alright with you all.

This will be all for the present. Hope to write again before the end of the week.

Very best love to Father, Mother, Millie and Laurie Dear,
From, Yrs. affectionately
"Theo"

Salvation Army Institute
Military Camp at
<u>Casula</u>
Jan. 10th 1915

Dear Teddie,
Just a scribble to let you know that I'm still alive, in good health and spirits and hope the same applies to you. I have meant to write before but kept saying that tomorrow night will do. Now I've started, here goes.

We entrained No.9 Platform, Adelaide on the 9th Dec. at 3.30 p.m., passed through Melbourne at noon next day and arrived at Liverpool in the morning at 8.30 on the 11th. A march of about 2 miles brought us to Casula. This is a new camp, with all tents situated on a tabletop hill, a fairly healthy place, but only the drainage system would make S.A. camp authorities crook for life. It will cause trouble, I'm thinking.

There are about 6,000 men here and about 10,000 in Liverpool camp on which we look down upon, it being on low lying ground on the other side of the River George. We've our full battalion strength, about 1,200. The N.S.W. and Queenies[12] form No.1 Company, Vic and S.A. No.2 and Tassies[13] and W.A. No.3 Company. We have more Officers than any other Battalion in the Service. I entered as a blacksmith, but rather than be left in the Reinforcements, I took on Officers Batman. I don't think that we'll live here much longer and believe we will see England to finish training. Our band started up last Thursday presented by some society in Melbourne. As a mascot we've a bulldog presented from somewhere, a sixty-pound (sterling) dog. The Methodists presented us with a recreation tent and someone or something else is giving a new piano. The crowd is pretty rough, miners mostly. They are all men though when the time comes, but for a few days after payday the drink has them all done in.

My two mates went to S.A. at Christmas and were due back on the 2nd. I didn't expect to see them back then either; they eventually turned up on the 8th. They've a good tale each to tell and I think they will get on alright. There is always an average of at least six missing. One fellow hasn't come away from S.A. yet. This is life here after quiet Adelaide; bands and bugles, concerts and games all around. Each week a crowd leave and of course some row is made.

Sydney is twenty-three miles from here. We never pay to

---

12 Queenslanders

13 Tasmanians

go in by train and there are some crowds on them sometimes; on platforms, steps and all over the engine, anywhere, as long as one gets there. Sydney is a fast place and everyone seems gay. The city itself has dirty streets, narrow, all twists and turns, up and down. The suburbs are clean, something like being back in Adelaide. I spent a very good time through the holidays visiting different places. I have been to Bronte, Coogee, Little Coogee, Cronulla, Balmoral, Lane Cove and Manly – mostly seaside resorts.

Am writing in the Salvation Army tent – rotten pens – one soon gets sick of writing and I've about 20 to write to. I heard from Len on the 29th and from Les on the 4th. They were both alright. I have not heard from Snook but heard that he had reached Egypt.

I will knock off now and write again soon, so hooray for the time and keep fit and smile on,

from,
Yours faithfully,
(Sgd.) W. Willmett.

Petersburg
May 8th, 1915

My dear All,
Very many thanks Laurel and Mother for your ever-welcome letters. Jove, Laurie, you are quite alright as a scribe. We will be having you launching out as a lady journalist yet.

The news about Father's success in the matter of work coming is particularly cheering. When the gardens come to fruition and the fruit trees are planted, when a picket fence takes the place of the hedge, Wright's home will be quite alright, eh, what?

Mother dear, Mrs. B. said that you remark that my letters were rather shorter than usual since my return. Perhaps they are, but I haven't noticed it; please bear in mind that most of my time when not at gym is spent home at my work-table – as a result I have nothing of interest usually to pass on.

Ivey tells me that her brother-in-law from Mannum has been called into camp. He held the rank of Captain prior to his resignation

Gym is going pretty strong. If the depression was not so acute I have no doubt that more would enrol for it, even though the sub amounts to only a trifling sum. I guess a good many have to refuse their youngsters although things are improving, for the railway employers have been put on fulltime again.

My sincere thanks Mother dear, for your loving remembrances re Ivey and self. I hope that things will work out alright some day. I am very glad that you all like Ivey. I can assure you that with her the feeling is mutual.

With regard to my wardrobe; it sadly needs replenishing and I would be very much obliged, Mother, if you would secure a pyjama suit for me, also a couple of fashion shirts, ordinary cuffs, neck 15-1/2. Please, did I leave a pair or two of socks behind? I'm short. Shall I forward you some cash or will you purchase and send me the account including the cost of replacing glass in the book-case, which I forgot for the time being. (Also a couple of undershirts.)

I don't go on duty 'til 1.30 today – things a bit slack.

Au Revoir now, dear Mother, Dad, Millie and Laurie, with fondest love to all,

Yours etc.,
"Theo"

<u>Petersburg</u>
Sunday 13-6-15
My dear All,

Well another of my flying trips is now a thing of the past, but I spent an enjoyable time. Thank you all, for all you did for me.

Well my watch was 15 minutes fast and so I arrived in town in heaps of time. On boarding the Payneham car I ran across an old Petersburg tennis pal, one Gordon Craig, who used to also play around at Walker's. We had a nice chat about old times; he is employed at the Islington Locomotive Workshops. It was nice for us to meet again.

By Jove, I had a cold trip. I simply could not get warm and I had refreshments at a number of places on the way. The country all the way up showed signs of having received good soaking rains and I guess that the crops and feed will now make excellent headway. The Cockies[14] and the Cattlemen seemed in excellent spirits at the prospects.

I went straight to work on arrival here and also worked that night and Wednesday and Thursday nights. So you see I have been pretty busily engaged. Did jobbing work Friday and Friday night I turned in pretty early.

Yesterday I was working again. I was down to play tennis in the afternoon but preferred to work. I had a good run till about 4 o'clock, when a delicate part broke and now will have to wait 'til tomorrow to be repaired by a jeweller. So I came home and had a bath.

Last evening I spent in an easy chair by the fire, I reckoned I had just about earned a good rest and it was A1 too. My word this is a cold place – heaps and heaps colder than the

---

14 Farmers

city. The sun is shining brightly today and, even so, 'tis very cold.

Mother dear, I am more convinced than ever that Ivey is the girl for me – somehow I get on far better with her than with other nice girls I have met.

I would like to be with the boys' class at Maughan Church today; it would be A1.

The Terowie boys did not, I am glad to say, visit us to play basketball last night. So that pleasure is still to come.

I start work at 8 a.m. tomorrow. Albert May left yesterday, so we now have his work to do in addition to our own.

I received a letter from Mr Clark and he asked if I was looking for a situation and saying that if I cared to return to the Mount he could make room for me. I think it is very kind of him and have written saying that I am willing to resume work under him if we can come to satisfactory terms, and asking him to let me know what my duties are likely to be, what wages he is prepared to pay, and when he would want me to go along. I wired him Saturday that I viewed the matter favourably; I was writing and the letter is now on the way and I expect to receive a reply by the end of the week. I have been waiting a long time for something to turn up and I believe Mr. Clark has a good chance to offer me; anyway if 'tis anything like a fair thing, I'm having a go at it.

It is rather funny that I should be offered a position there about the same time as you were negotiating with a buyer for the house.[15] I am glad that you are selling the old home, for I don't think it would be a wise thing for you all to return; you would be too dissatisfied with your limited surroundings after the unlimited scope which the city offers, and, too, the city seems to agree with all of you. As for myself I have not

---

15 Theo's parents sold their Mount Gambier house after they moved to Adelaide

had a sufficient spell in the city for a return to the Mount to make much difference, and I really think it is a chance to advance, which is offering.

I guess I will, if I return, get a bad time from all the old pals and relations for not writing, but I guess that will soon be overcome. I sent Clark the paper, which I had the most responsibility of producing, and also a copy of the following week's issue containing my 'Empire Day' report, which might mean a bob or two more for me.

Yes, I haven't any interest to speak of in tennis now. On Saturday last I made my debut at the rifle range; the distances were 800 and 900 yards (half a mile), and the first two shots which I fired were bullseyes, but I got off the target a bit after that at 800; at 900 yards, however, I shot pretty consistently scoring 28 out of a possible 50. They reckoned it was good for my first shoot, especially as it was the old type of rifle such as we used in the Senior Cadets, which I had to use, while the others had the modern pattern.

Yes, Mother, dear the *Times* has been a heavy proposition lately and last Friday's was a daisy but we are rubbing along fairly well. Night work and overtime such as I have been putting in of late, however, is over the fence, especially for a pittance of two pounds and 5 shillings a week which little more than keeps things moving. I'm worse off now than when we left the Mount.

I must turn in now. Don't say anything about the Mt. G. offer until a settlement is assured.

With love to all,
Yours lovingly,
"Theo"

AUSTRALIAN MILITARY FORCES
4th MILITARY DISTRICT
Recruiting Office,
Keswick,

15.6.15

Mr. T. W. Wright,
"Times" Office,
Petersburg.

Sir,
In reply to your letter of 13th. Inst., I have to inform you that
the regulation regarding artificial teeth is still in force.

Unless a man has good sound natural back teeth sufficient
to masticate his food he cannot be accepted.

Yours faithfully
(Sgd.) C. Floodways
Captain.
Enrolling Officer

Petersburg
Sunday 20-6-15

My very dear 'Quartet',
I am afraid my news will be very scarce this week, for there is
very little doing besides work!

Gymnasium occupied my time on Tuesday and Wednesday
evenings. We did not have a very good time, for those who
know the work and could help us won't come along, in spite
of promises to do so. Interest is therefore slackening for what
I know isn't much. Still, we are going to try and keep going.

Thursday I was at it hammer and tongs and finished fifteen

minutes after midnight. I worked Friday, but yesterday my machine went to the pack, so I had to dismantle, clean, and put it in order again. However, 'tis going bonnily again, so that isn't so bad, eh.

Friday night I had a two hour talk here in me little wooden 'ut, with a chap from the South-East, a Mr. Percy Hilton, whose father is head keeper at Cape Banks lighthouse. He, with his wife, is at Mr. Day's next door for a day or two. He is a carpenter at Terowie. We had quite an interesting talk re the old spots down there and different sports. He and his family, it transpired, had a telephone acquaintance with Fred. They used to call him *Little Fred*!

Yesterday afternoon I had a contest with Tiny in connection with the ladder scheme of the Petersburg Club. Everyone thought it would prove an easy victory for Gerlach, and he promised not to give me a harder licking than 6-0, 6-0. Very kind of him, eh. But I made him feel rather foolish – after him talking so much – for he only won by 1 solitary game out of 3 sets. I won the first 6-5, and he the next two 6-5, 6-5, he getting 17 games and I 16. It was a long way from being good tennis. I should have won, though. It was this way – I had him 5-1 in the first and then only just got in with 6 to 5, in the second we were even to 5 all and deuce. It was then my advantage and I thought to end the set with a smashing volley, but I hit it out; that brought us back to deuce again, and I lost the next two strokes – leaving Tiny the winner of that by a game. There's not much excuse for me not winning the 3rd set for I was 4 to 1, but he made it 5 all and won. He was disgusted. We others went on to football but he was in a bad humour and went home.

I actually enjoyed an evening at the pictures last night. It was a bonnie programme and I'm glad I went.

I guess it was nice to have Con and the kiddies down for a couple of days. Did Dad go to the Mount?

So father has the offer of more work – that sounds good! Yes, Mill, I believe the girls do have fun with the little folk at Kindergarten.

Work is going pretty well, thanks and I am A.1. again. When will you have time to write again, Mother dear? Did I tell you that I wrote to military headquarters last Sunday re joining the forces? Have been informed that false teeth regulation is still in force. So I can't go yet.

Write soon. I haven't any more 'noos'[16] so will close.

Heaps of love to all from,

"Ted".

Petersburg
Monday, 26-7-15

My dear All,

Your P.C.[17] to hand on Saturday Mill, and yours, Mother and Father and Laurie today; many thanks for them. I am sure Dave Badger would be glad for the fruits of your industry in knitting. On Friday night, I too bought *For King and Empire* and was able to pick out some of the fellows whom I knew: Alan and Curly Schramm being the principal ones. It is a very well produced piece of work.

There's something doing here on Australia Day as you will have noticed by our last issue of *Times*; but it is making a great deal more work for us and no extra pay – which stings. My colleague is tired of the game and turned it up on Saturday last; he is trying to get in the locomotive shops

---

16 news

17 Post Card

and went to town today to be examined. Bennett has lost no time in getting someone to take his place for a man is to arrive by tonight's express; but things won't be the same without Len. (Learnt at dance that Len passed and starts at loco. tomorrow.)

I am hoping that he will soon have to get a man to succeed yours truly.

Love
"Theo"

PS. Accompanied by two of the boys I did thirty miles on the bike yesterday afternoon after working all the morning. The country looks beautiful, such a contrast to a few months back.

AUSTRALIAN MILITARY FORCES
4th MILITARY DISTRICT

Enrolling Office,
Keswick, 18/7/15

Mr T.W.WRIGHT
"Times" Office
Petersburg

Dear Sir,

In reply to your letter of the 7th inst. regarding the eligibility of persons having a full set of artificial teeth for enlistment in the Australian Imperial Force.

I regret to inform you that under no circumstances can a Person with a full set of artificial teeth be accepted, even if a duplicate set is obtained.

Yours Faithfully
(Sgd.)
Captain.
Enrolling Officer.

<u>Petersburg</u>
Aug.15, 1915
Dear All,

Thank you all for the letters received this week – it was just bonnie to receive them. Jove, I'm looking forward to coming home again for a while.

Tiny and I walked to Yongala this morning and we have not long since arrived home. We have had a bonza time. Tell you about it when I see you later on. Yesterday I went down by train and played tennis with them for the afternoon. Worked last night and expect to do the same every night this coming week.

What do you think? Bennett came to light with a 5 bob rise Friday; I could hardly believe my eyes! I've put in to leave Saturday next, Father, and will be able to do so if boss can make his arrangements. I will let you know the result later on. It will mean the loss of a week's wages, though, upon which I was counting a lot!

Hope to see Strath folks. Will just catch the mail if I hurry. More anon.

Yours lovingly,
"Theo"

<u>Petersburg</u>
Aug.20, 1915

Dear Father, and all,

I received your card Wednesday Dad. So I did, and do, want to get away from the Burg as soon as possible, but circumstances, as usual, are against me. As I gave Bennett notice for next Saturday and as his arrangements have not been finalised – I know that he has done his best for I've been shaking him up all the time – I will have to stay on here till next Saturday, and the coming week will be a very long one for this chick. I expect to leave here on Monday the 30th, and will arrive in town somewhere about 10 am, if I can catch the 3 a.m. express. As I will now be there over the Sunday of that week Frank Ward has very kindly asked me to put in the weekend with them and I expect so to do. I will be working all hours this coming week I expect for I have a show prize list to turn out in addition to the ordinary work. But never mind, 'twill be the LAST!

Frank and Nellie and two young ladies came up on Wednesday last and played tennis at Walker's and I managed to get off too. As it was an ideal day we had a bonnie time and Mrs. W and Trix regaled us with refreshments. They had received a letter from Hurtle, who has so far come right through the Dardanelles' operations without any hurt. I accepted Mr. Walker's invite to stay and have tea, and afterwards went on duty and worked till 1 a.m. Put in another strenuous day yesterday, but left off at about 10 p.m. I didn't trouble to turn out 'til 10 this morning and so am a bit behind today – however I reckon I've done my bit.

I suppose the Strath. Folks will be home by the time I get down; what bad luck, I wanted very much to see them. Never mind I might be able to manage a day up there!

It's very kind of you, Dad, to offer me remuneration for what I may do for you. That had not entered my head; but if you are in a position to do so, I guess the same will be acceptable, and many thanks for the offer.

You may think me foolish, but I expect to be again examined by the doc., tomorrow night. Another of my pals will go down to camp today week. He informed me on his return the other day that they are not nearly so strict as regards teeth now. I would sooner go into camp than go back to the Mount! Of course if I happened to pass it would be necessary for me to get leave to fix up with Clark …[18]

W. H. BENNETT
PRINTER & PUBLISHER
PETERSBURG TIMES

TO WHOM IT MAY CONCERN

The Bearer, Theo W. Wright, has been in our employ for over two years as a monoline operator and during that period proved himself a very reliable and willing workman, doing his utmost at all times to assist in the many difficulties that arise in newspaper work. When hard pressed, he has assisted in the composing and machinery department and altogether we found most useful in the office generally. We can confidently recommend him to anyone requiring his service. He leaves us of his own accord and we regret that he is severing his connection with this office.

(Sgd W. H. Bennett)
Proprietor.

---

18 The final page of this letter is missing.

Mount Gambier
Sunday 19-9-15

My dearest All,
Your letters to hand yesterday and many thanks for them, it was good to hear from you.

Did you receive the balance of the money for the Walkerville contract[19], Father; I do hope that you have.

I have had a very quiet time this week, and have been working well, eating well, sleeping well and am feeling very fit as a result. Two fellow boarders and I do physical exercises every night that it is practicable - we are making it a part of the daily routine, and as we are able to indulge in the luxury of a shower, it is A.1.

One of my fellow boarders, Tommy Williams, has been ill with tonsillitis since Thursday last. I have been a bit of a nurse, doing odd jobs for him, including making his bed. He reckons he could recommend me as a nurse. I spent practically the whole of yesterday afternoon with him; I guess it was a bit of a break in the monotony to have someone to talk to.

Last night I went down the street for a while and met a number of friends and relations and had several pleasant chats – was walking up and down the street for about half an hour with Frank Carr. Today I was there to dinner and had a real good time. They all asked after you and wished to be remembered.

This afternoon we attended the memorial service to the soldiers who fell in the South African War, which was held at the

---

19 Theo's father, Joseph Wright worked as a builder and was reliant for income from contracts for building services.

Memorial. Several hymns were sung, Archdeacon Samwell[20] gave an address, buglers sounded *The Last Post* and relatives of the fallen men placed wreaths at the foot of the memorial, after which the band rendered the National Anthem and proceedings came to an end. It was an impressive ceremony.

It was too wet for a constitutional this morning. We three boys had a singsong after breakfast and then went to church, so I consider that we have been good.

I hope that you received basket and rug; I paid the delivery fee for same.

I had a chat with Uncle Jim last night. He has cut away limbs from a tree. He has seen Mr. Hosking about the dresser, but he says I can collect money now. I will see to that this week and the rental of the paddock and also will make enquiries re felling of tree.

Working at the *Star* is child's play compared to what I put in at Petersburg. I reckon I'll be about twice as big when I come home again eh what? Everyone exclaims as to how I've grown; Constable Haldane did not know me at first and when he did recognise me he said, 'You've grown crossways as well as taller'.

Aunt Mary expects Win home tomorrow. I am going up there on Wednesday. Last Sunday was a bonza day, but it has been very squally ever since; real Mount Gambier weather.

'Tis now 9.30 p.m. so I must be off to the pillar[21] with these, and then get between the sheets, ready for another good day's work tomorrow.

---

20 One of the first to leave for the front from Petersburg was Archdeacon Samwell, Rector of the St Peters Anglican Church. He was the first Army Chaplain ever appointed in South Australia. http://www. peoplesvoice.gov.au/stories/sa/peterborough/peterborough_w_ww1.htm

21 Pillar Box – PostBox

So, *Au Revoir* with fondest love to each and all.
Yours etc.,
"Theo"

  Mount Gambier,
Oct. 24th, 1915

Dear Mill,
I received your bonnie long letter dated 13th; also the card enclosed with Dad's letter received last Wednesday. I reckon, the photo is bonnie, Mill; you make a good boy. Didn't you feel shy when being snapped? This is my sixth letter today – going strong, am I not?

I guess you were disappointed at not having your walk; I would not have disappointed you, I'm sure.

You girls seem to have good times together. I wish I could have been a member of the party that went to the St. Peter's concert! Say, Mill, are you not now glad I became acquainted with Ivey and Olive? Do you remember that you were not going to have anything to do with them? See what good times and pals you would have missed!

I guess the two Kids did have a good time at West's. You are a stop out when you are making a night of it. You are nearly as bad as I.

I have just been talking to Myra. She is just the same as ever. She tells me that she has a photo of Allan for me. I'm so very glad, for I was wondering if the old boy would remember me.

I have been a good boy tonight; having just arrived home from church. Horace Haddy was there; camp life has done him a power of good, he looks quite big.

Say, Mill don't be surprised if Trixie Walker drops in to see you one of these days. I told her when I was there to drop in and give you a call if she was in town at any time. I am sure you will like her, Mill; be nice to her and take her out home with you if possible. As you know, Walkers were very, <u>very</u> good to me while I was in the 'Burg and if ever you do meet Trix, and do as I ask, you will be doing me a kindness too. I am glad you correspond with Dolly Oates, she's a gay old kid and not a bad sort at all.

Yesterday afternoon the Red Cross girls had stalls at different positions in the street and sold all sorts of things. I bought a couple of bottles of cool drink from Consie Billing, and from the flower girls a great bunch of picotees.[22] Mill Clark has promised to pack 'em for me so that I can send you along some flowers. Now, they are not all for you folks, you must share them with Ivey. If Mill C. keeps her promise they ought to leave by tomorrow evening's train. If they do so, they will be addressed to Mother; I will drop a note to Ivey and she can come out to you for some if she desires to.

I am going to get Mr. B. to take my photo on Wed.; if so will send you along one at the end of the week. By the way, did I leave that P.C. of Trix W. and the other two P'burg soldier girls at home? I have lost track of it. If you find it please send it along.

Ted's pal must have liked your company alright. Roy Underwood is also here on long leave; likewise Rupert Wilson, but I have only spoken a few words to them. I always feel mighty sore and dissatisfied when I see these other chaps off to do their bit – and I <u>can't</u> go!

You two kids had a lively time after all on Anzac Day. 'Tis well to be some people! What price, Les Opie being engaged; don't let on if the girls have not told you!

I received a letter from the Rash boy about a fortnight ago. Do you see much of him?

---

22 A type of carnation flower.

Carving is going strong; I am in love with the work and hope to do a bit for <u>my</u> 'glory box', eh what!

This is all for this trip. Write another such bonnie letter soon.

Lots-o'-love from
"Theo"

AUSTRALIAN MILITARY FORCES
4th MILITARY DISTRICT
Recruiting Depot, Currie St, Adelaide

Dear Sir,

In reply to your letter of 25th. Inst.[23] I have to inform you that if you have a complete set of artificial teeth, you would not be passed as 'Fit' for Active Service.

Yours Faithfully
(Sgd.) G. R. Corpe
Lieut.
Enrolling Officer

Mr. T. W. Wright
Star Office,
MOUNT GAMBIER
SOUTH AUSTRALIA.
Nov. 28th 1915

Dearest Mother, and Father and youngsters,

Do you know, I wrote to Dad on Friday during the dinner hour and – forgot to post it? I'm sorry, but my brain-box has been very busy of late with one thing and another and I have been forgetting all sorts of things. For instance, last night I meant

---

23 It was popular at that time to contract instant to inst and actually pronounce the word inst.

to get writing materials and see about my paper, which has not been delivered lately, and I forgot; so to-day I have had to borrow a pad from Will; that's why the quality of the paper is so good.

I received a very nice letter on Wednesday night from the I. C. S., covering three pages and advising me on which courses of study would be useful to me. They recommend advertising or gas-power and motor engineering; the latter course does not attract me and I think I shall take on the former. They also expressed regret at my inability to keep up to the terms of the agreement and hoped that I would soon be able to send along a part of my arrears, at any rate, and that my circumstances would speedily improve. They are treating me very well and I hope to soon to get matters straightened up and get going with the advertising course.

As you know, I think, the *Border Watch*[24] have, since the fire, installed intertype machines, which are practically the same as the linotype. Mr. Will Chesterfield is the chief one with these machines and he and I had a chat about them one day. As a result he is putting me in the way of getting two books, which will be of immense value, I think, as a lift in the direction of the lino.[25] Mr. Chesterfield is very kind to take an interest in me; I value it all the more because he was the first to broach it. Mr. C. is going to help me all he can, but I must be careful not to fall out with Mr. Clark; he may take it into his head that I am putting in with the *Watch*. So this is just between ourselves you know. I went around to Mr. C. last night and he lent me a book to look over today, entitled, *The mechanism of the linotype*, and I intend buying a book (although costly; 'tis worth its weight in gold) and we are sending for two other books dealing with

24 Competing paper to *The Star.*

25 Linotype a machine that produces a solid 'line of type' introduced about 1886. It was used for generations by newspapers and general printers.

the work. It's every man for himself these days, and I am not letting slip any opportunity where the lino is concerned.

Len Carr and I went for a horseback ride on Sunday. I had a colt from McDonough's. Besides being young it had been in the stable for a fortnight, so you can imagine there was something doing. However, I had <u>NOT</u> forgotten the way to sit a horse and although he plunged about for a start and was all over the road at times, I liked it all the more and had a real joy ride. I hired the colt again yesterday afternoon, and had even more fun for a start; he was <u>so</u> fresh, first on his forelegs and then on his hind legs, doing a bit of a see-saw and cavorting around. He's a dear and just playful and not a bit vicious. I was out four hours and had a lovely ride. I wish I could buy the horse. I hope to have one some day soon! I'm not stiff at all today.

I went to the Methodist picnic on Wednesday and had a good time, but it was awful without the boys, especially Alan. There seemed hardly any of the old chums at all.

Last night I went to the pictures with Frank and Arthur Carr;[26] Frank is a grass widower for a fortnight. Really, I am great pals with Carr's, and have good times with the boys and Harvey Timby. Little Edna is a love. I go up to Palmers' every Tuesday and Friday evening with a paper and to say good-day, so I am not allowed to get lonely. I also see Aunt Jane now and then; it was her birthday last Sunday and I forgot. I'm rather afraid to go and see her, she's sure to give me some good breaks.

I was disappointed at not getting a letter last night. Things don't seem the same unless I get my home love-letter.

How are the Wolseley folk getting on in their new surroundings?

What's happened to Daisy? 'Tis ages since I have heard from her! Flo Wright has been to Strathalbyn; she saw Fred and said he was A1. And she was praising up young Glen.[27]

---

26 The Carr family are cousins to the Wright family.

27 Fred and Evelyn are the 'Strath Folk' and Glen is their oldest child

Fancy, Australia wants 50,000 more men. There may be a chance for me yet.

Hurry up and write, please!

Heaps of love from Yours Lovingly,

"Theo"

Mount Gambier
Midnight
Monday, 20 December 1915

Dearest Mother and All,

I wanted to send a note by the early mail, but was unable to do so. I wrote you a fairly long letter on Wednesday last telling you that I regretted that I would not be able to come home for Xmas as we only get Saturday and Monday off. As you have not replied, I am wondering if you received it or not. I am very disappointed at not being able to come, you bet. Ivey is disappointed also, but it can't be helped.

Within the next day or so a case will arrive, out home, addressed to Mother. It contains my Xmas box to you all at home, and I hope it will give you as much joy in the receiving as it does me in the sending. The case was to leave by 'goods' today midday and would go to Mile End, and as it was addressed to Mother at Evandale, etc. the carrier would deliver it from Mile End. I was advised not to pay the delivery rate as they might get at me both ends, so please fix it up and let me know what it cost you as soon as possible. Once more, I express the hope that you will be pleased with the contents of the case.

As far as I now know I shall spend the holidays with Carr's at the Bay, where we will put up at the Victoria Hotel. I expect to help Carr's a bit on Xmas Eve – probably at the till.

Received a letter from Dais tonight, which has been long delayed. She seems to be having a good time, doesn't she?

I hope to hear from some of you in a day or two.

Father will probably have a better time on the letter round this year than last; that is if you are experiencing the cool weather that is prevailing here.

Received a photo of Glen Wright the other day. It was A.1.

Hoo-roo everybody – Don't eat too many delicacies and do think of me!

Best of wishes from,

Yours lovingly –

"Theo"

1916

Racecourse Camp
Heliopolis
12/1/1916

Dear Theo,
So glad to get your letters. I wrote a card to you before we left for the front - suppose you have it by this time. It must be rotten for you not being able to get away. Never mind old chap, after all somebody must stay home. It's hard luck it could be you though. It is jolly fine seeing all these places. I go out with two nurses a good lot. I knew them in Adelaide and they are very decent girls. They took me out visiting last Sunday afternoon and at night we had dinner in Cairo and then went to a wedding. It was different to Australian weddings but I was jolly glad to see it. Was introduced to a nice little girl and she was explaining it to me. Got home about 1 a.m. Reg Carr is in this Regiment. It is just about time for parade. When we first came back it was very cold here but the last few days have been bonza. How are things doing in the Mount? Pretty slow, I'll bet. Remember me to all the boys please. I am in real good health. Was on Gallipoli about a fortnight. Give my love to all your people.
Your old Cobber
Alan.

Mount Gambier
Feb. 20th, 1916[28]
My dearest All,

Your cards received and many thanks for them. I knew it would not be a very great surprise to you to learn that I had got through

28 This was written the day before the Battle of Verdun opened.

for the war. I got through 'flying' and Mr. Engelbrucht, who is the dental examining officer, assures me that I won't have any difficulty in getting through – at least that was with the set of teeth I had on Tuesday last. Now, you will wonder why I say that! Well, without any beating about the bush, I'll tell you. I lost my new set at the river on Wednesday last, after taking them out before swimming, too! I swam about longer than the others and cramp seized me just as I was getting out owing to the cold current near the bank. I got into the boat and when my clothes were passed I did not think about my teeth, as my leg was cramped, and the blanky things fell out of my pocket into the water. Of course I dived for 'em, but to no purpose. On my appearance back at our party there were cries of consternation and much sympathy, but that didn't bring my 'ivories' back.

I managed pretty well for tucker, but had to eat with my back to the assembled company. After dinner we returned to the fatal spot and I spent a lot of time and energy in diving. I did not expect to retrieve them, but of course I had to make an attempt.

Alf Aconley also had a mishap; he went into mud up to his knees and it took several of us to haul him out. They dubbed us the two Jonahs. Mrs. Will Jaeger took a snapshot of Alf and myself – 'The Jonah's' – and one of the boys stood behind the camera and made me laugh, so that I will be a pretty looking object. We had a lovely time that day in spite of all the ill luck. I have not told you who the party consisted of: Mr. & Mrs. Will Jaeger, Mrs. Tormay and her two boys and daughter, Mr. & Mrs. Hirth, Misses Roughan (2), Clark (2), Aconley, Messrs. Spail, Pat McMahon and Alf Aconley. Frank Jaeger had obtained permission to go, and of course, I could not go also. But on hearing that I intended going to camp, Frank told me on Tuesday night to take his place. Of course I was delighted. However, I'm not quite broke yet, and I still have a kick left in me, but my ill luck is past understanding, isn't it? …

Mount Gambier
20th February 1916

Dear Cousins,

Here we are again. I am quite happy now for I passed the military test 'flying' on Tuesday last and leave here on the morning of the 28th and expect to go into camp next day. Isn't it bully? 'Tis time I had a bit of luck, isn't it? So it's me for a soldier's life now, Hurrah – rah - rah ! But what do you think has happened to me since Xmas – I've lost two bally sets of teeth, both as the result of being so fond of swimming. The first set I lost in the Valley Lake soon after Xmas. I then got a 12 guinea set and they were absolutely perfect. Last Wednesday I went with a party to the Glenelg River.[29] Of course some of us went swimming. This time I put my 'ivories' into my pocket for safety. When I had finished and was handling my clothes the d---- things fell out of the boat into deep water. I spent a lot of time and energy diving for them but hadn't any luck. Am I not a 'Jonah' altogether?

Do you ever play tennis now? I have had two games with a borrowed racket, but did not enjoy them much. So you are going to Henley, coz Nell. I hope I will see you while I am down. Please give my very kindest regards to Hilda H. and tell her I may be able to get her a Turkish fez[30] yet – if I ever meet the Turcos[31] now.

I have been too excited lately to settle down to anything and I don't seem to have any news even now.

I have had a pretty gay time down here; and work has been

29 Glenelg River near Mt Gambier at Nelson.

30 Felt cap shaped like a flat topped cone.

31 Turkish. Obviously Theo wanted to fight the Turkish in reprisal for Gallipoli

going bonza. Have had a beautiful run with my machines here for a couple of months or more. Different to the old tub, which I used to work at the 'Burg, eh?

Well, ta, ta! For this time. Give Gladys and Jean a kiss for me please and tell Jean I'm off after the Germans.

"Au Revoir"
Love from Ted.

Machine Gun Section
Morphetville
30th May 1916

Dear Cousins,
Here goes at last for a letter to you, which it has been for some time my intention to write. My excuse for not having written is lack of time and I can tell you I am a jolly busy chap.

It was bonza to see you, Frank, when you were down and I was mighty sorry we could only say practically 'hullo' and 'goodbye'!

I am so sorry, coz Nell that I missed you and the kiddies when you were down in February. You see Frank told me the date of your return home and as that was the day I went into camp, I could not see you. He, however said when I saw him Easter that you had extended your holiday. How I wish I had known. I wanted to take a run up to see you, but as I had to get such a lot done in the comparatively short time we had on leave, I couldn't possibly manage it. Yes the Hicks family were holidaying at Moonta for Easter. I met Bert Hodby at Mitcham.

Tell Jean it was lovely to read her little letter and the drawings were A1. I was specially flattered at Glady's effort. Aren't children good fun, eh?

We have attended several big functions lately. A play was

presented to the 23rd Battalion by the Glenelg[32] Church and after the ceremony refreshments were provided by the ladies and I can tell you the looking after a whole battalion was a big item, but they treated us right royally.

Last Thursday the Governor-General inspected the 23rd and incidentally pulled our legs a great deal. We boys were looking forward to 'general leave' as a result, but were doomed to disappointment – there was 'nothing doing'.

To-day 'tis pouring with rain and the 'heads' gave us the day off to make our final business arrangements. A special train and ditto trams conveyed us to the city. You bet everyone will make the best of it, but I guess there will be a number of 'drunks' wending their way to camp tonight. I was nearly concluding without telling you the date of our departure. We embark on the 9th June and judging by the Governor-General's remarks the other day, ultimate destination will be the Western Front – in Flanders. They will be stirring times then, I guess!

I forgot to say the *Adelaide Cheer-up Society* [33] is giving us a 'bang-up' send off in the Exhibition Building tomorrow night. Sure, we will have a good time – eh what?

Must bid you a 'fond farewell' now and conclude with again thanking you for your great kindness to me when I was up North.

Love to all.

Yours sincerely

THEO

---

32 Glenelg in Adelaide not the town near Mt Gambier

33 The Adelaide Cheer-up Society planned dances and parties; also they organised memorials.

Morphetville
8-6-16

My dearest Mother, Father and Sisters,
I thought I would write a few lines today and post the letter so that you would perhaps receive it after I had gone on board the boat.

Although I feel sad at the thoughts of leaving you all, I am quite contented. I feel that I am doing my bit and hope that the 43rd will make a reputation for itself over yonder.

Don't worry about me at all, I am able to look after myself and am quite prepared for anything that may come to pass.

Don't forget, Mother dear, if ever you should need any of the money that you bank for me, you are to use it. Also if Ivey should be in any difficulty at any time I would like you to help her if you can. She talks of going away to the country somewhere, but whether she will or not remains to be seen.

I consider myself well blessed to have such bonza parents and brother and sisters and I love you all dearly; you may often think that I have a funny way of showing it, and it will be a happy day if I am spared to come back to you.

Whatever happens 'tis my intention to play the game in everything and not give you any cause for sorrow.

If I go under, dear ones, don't be sorrowful, for <u>I am not afraid to go</u>; I haven't been an angel by any means, but I've tried to play the game.

Au Revoir, everyone!
Yours Lovingly
"Theo"

On Active Service
'At Sea'[34]
My dear Home-folks,

By Jove, it seems an age since we left home. The fact that
we have not received any letters makes the time seem much
longer. We are all looking forward to the time when we will
receive our first mail; that is a very long way off yet! However,
I'll have to learn to be patient – a lesson that would not do me
any harm eh?

Time passes pleasantly enough. Among such a number of
high-spirited chaps, there's sure to be plenty of fun, you know.
And we do have fun, too! Boxing is a favourite pastime with
our section and no day passes without a number of bouts with
the gloves. I like the game very much and would like to become
good at it. The 'heads' are drawing up a sports programme and
there should be lots o' fun in store for us. We are continuing
our training as far as possible on board ship and the days on
which we work are the best days for they pass quickly and we
are benefited by them, whereas, it is a slow old game idling
about.

I wonder did you receive my wire, letter and views, which
were sent from Albany. I sincerely hope you did. To judge by
the views you will be thinking that we must have spent rather a
delightful time. But we had only about an hour to look around
and that time was spent buying up and having a good tuck in at
a fish shop. To start from the beginning…

A few days sailing brought us in sight of land and during
one day we gradually drew closer into a hilly coast until we
entered a strait and then on into Albany Harbour. The passage

---

34 The date has been blotted out by the censor

up the strait to Albany is rather picturesque and very rugged. The town itself is spread out between and on the slopes of two prominent hills and is prettily situated. On coming in sight of port the boys began bustling about sprucing themselves up in anticipation of a trip ashore, but they were doomed to disappointment for that day and were forced to appreciate Albany's charms from a distance. And the view from the boat was quite charming enough to make one wish he were able to make a close acquaintance. The hills made me long for a good old ramble amongst them, like we used to do down at the Mount. We were allowed ashore the morning after our arrival, but it was in the form of a route march in which all the battalion took part. We were early astir and breakfast was over by 7 a.m.; an hour or two after, a column of khaki-clad figures wound its way from the ship, along the wharf and over a long hill into the town, with a couple of military bands to stir us up. We were given a good welcome and on arrival at the Town Hall were dismissed, as I previously mentioned. We returned by the same route and the ship sailed on her way again at midday. The visit formed a pleasant break in our journey and it was good to be able to stretch our legs on terra firma once again.

After leaving Albany the weather began to get warmer and the sea not so rough and conditions have been better than was previously the case.

(This paragraph has been blotted out by the censor.)

How are you all keeping – exceedingly well I hope. You know none of you must worry about me; that won't do any good. I am quite able to look after myself and am having a very good time. I am anxiously awaiting news of Fred and trust that he has taken a turn for the better and is becoming his old self once again. You are all always in my thoughts; I am looking forward to receiving quite a pile of letters when the mail comes to hand one of these fine days.

We get plenty of music, which is provided by two brass bands, not to mention sundry instruments among the chaps, and some good deck concerts have been held. So far the food has been good and we have few grievances; of course conditions would be better if we were not so crowded, but nothing else could be expected. I can sleep pretty well in the ship's hammock.

The S.A. Government very considerately put on board 300 or so cases of apples for our use on the voyage and I can tell you they are very acceptable indeed. We get some every day, then we have the canteen to go to for any little luxuries; altogether, you know, we are having an alright time.

With every assurance of my good health and spirits, and the hope that you are all in good health also and that everything is going well at home and with the married ones,

I remain –
Your loving son and brother,
"Theo"

On Active Service
'Somewhere at Sea'
Lance Corpl. Theo Wright
Machine Gun Section

My dearest Homefolks –
I got tired of the everlasting sea on the trip from Colombo to Port Said; it seemed an age from the time we left Ceylon on the horizon until the desolate shores that bound the Red Sea came into sight. There was just one long range of mountains stretching for many, many miles; with the sea breaking at their feet, and these hills were absolutely bare of everything. On reaching Suez we stopped for a few hours some distance offshore, and then entered the canal.

The passage through this marvellous waterway was full of

interest; one side was cultivated and pleasant to the eye, while the other was just the extreme opposite – bare, sandy waste. The nights now are moonlight and this added to the beauty of the scene as we passed slowly through. The boys were too much taken up with things to think of sleep for some time after the usual hour of retiring.

You must understand that owing to strict censorship many things, which would add to your interest in my letter this time, have been prohibited and I can only touch lightly on some of the things I have seen during the past few days. Others I cannot mention at all, but I may be able to relate them at some future date. Of course the boys had something to say to all whom we passed and I bet those people knew by their repartee where the boys hailed from.

I forgot to mention that while in the Red Sea some of the soldiers, and officers too, had a go at assisting the stokers, as during the extreme heat of a day or two it was too much for them. It was a novelty to do this kind of work - a very little in that line goes a long way with me. At first I was shovelling coal from the bunkers to where it goes to the stokehold, and an hour's hard work it was. On being relieved I paid a visit to the stokehold[35] and watched and assisted a little in the process of feeding the great furnaces. The heat was very great; half an hour or so was enough there. I visited the engine room where the giant engines thundered and the heat was almost stifling.

My word I knew very little about what the men down below had to put up with before; now I have a slight conception of what their work entails and sympathise with them accordingly. Of course during our work in the 'black regions' we had picked up a good layer of coal dust and sweat from top to toe. It took

---

35 stokehold - chamber or compartment in which the furnaces of a ship are stoked or fired.

almost as long to get that off as it did to accomplish our little bit below.

To go back a little way:

The canal opens out at the mouth at Port Said, and here we anchored for a couple of days or so. It was not long before coaling and watering operations, such as took place at Colombo, were again in full swing, and the ship was swarming with niggers. There was no breeze and the coal dust settled over everything; the perspiration made it stick well and good, until everyone appeared the same hue as the niggers themselves. The first morning some of us went swimming; the water did not look too clear, but a swim was such a luxury that I went overboard and of course had a good bath afterwards. I swam across to a boat that was anchored near us and had a yarn with the sailors. I enjoyed my short visit immensely. We were not allowed to go ashore there and the time passed slowly and very uncomfortably owing to the coal dust and intense heat. Therefore I, at least, was not sorry when we left Port Said behind.

Yesterday and today have been much cooler and conditions are more comfortable. I think I told you in a previous letter about the mascots that are on board – a kangaroo and teddy bear. The latter is a nocturnal animal, that is, he sleeps during the day and plays high jinks in the night-time. Last night, for instance, while sleeping on deck, I was awakened by something soft jumping about on me. I found Teddy doing a tango. Then he ran off and climbed a rope to another place and left me in peace. I have only seen the little beggar in the daytime and thought he was a lazy stupid-looking animal, but last night I altered my opinion of him. Really, though, he is a funny little chap, and I bet the kiddies and Laurie would love to see him.

I can't think of any more news, the days are pretty much the same, you know. I'm sure I shall be glad to get to work on shore once again; a holiday is right enough, but too much ease also gets a bit wearisome. Not that I am having a bit of a grouse, you know, for we have very little to do and plenty of time to do it in. The tucker is as good as can be expected, and I am in excellent health, therefore there's no room to growl. A letter or two from home would make all the difference. The anticipation of the big 'budget'[36] that is coming one of these days, and the frequent perusal of some old ones which I have with me, helps me to wait with a little bit of patience for the mail. It's rather a comedown to go so many weeks without a letter after getting one on an average of every day.

Good-bye, everyone, with fondest love and heaps of kisses from
Your loving son and brother,
"Theo"

On Active Service
Lark Hill Camp[37]
12-7-16
To:
Lewis Gun Officer
43rd Battn.

With reference to deficiency of Lewis Gun spare parts of No.8 Platoon "B" Coy, I wish to report as follows: - Pte. F. E. Dyer and myself were told to accompany limber containing the magazines of "B" Coy. which were put on 30th Batt. Limber.[38] Thinking to look after them better we took with us our Lewis Gun and spare parts. En route from trenches, a party of wounded asked for assistance. We jumped off the limber in order to give what help we could. Meanwhile the limber had continued on and when we arrived at 30th Q.M. store we found

---

36 A quantity of written or printed material.

37 Salisbury Plain, England.

38 A two-wheeled, horse-drawn vehicle used to tow a field gun or a caisson.

that the contents of the limber had been transferred to 43rd Batt. limber. On arrival at our battalion camp, the spare parts (complete) were found to be missing; their deficiency and the cause thereof I hereby report.

Theo Willard Wright

Salisbury Plain,
England.
3-8-16
My dearest Loved Ones,
Continuing on from what I wrote in my last letter.

From Port Said a destroyer gave us protection and, you bet, a close watch was kept out for subs. However, we had a peaceable passage and arrived at Marseilles on a Thursday night, six weeks after the time of leaving the Outer Harbour. All was excitement on board the ship; the boys got up to tricks and little sleep was to be got that night. From the ship we could distinguish the blurred outline of the coast, with the beams of lighthouses regularly cutting the darkness. I got to sleep at last but was up again at 4 a.m.

We were shrouded in fog and it was long before it lifted to show us the beautiful city of Marseilles. The postcards, which I sent you, will give you an idea of the beauty of the scene. Terraces of beautiful buildings, many of quaint architecture, numerous large buildings which stood out in prominent parts of the hills, forts, hotels and chateaux, etc, with a generous sprinkling of gardens and vineyards. From the harbour we could trace the line of the railway, where it climbed the mountains – over viaducts and bridges, and through tunnels. You will notice the breakwater, fort and other notable features in those views and they will help you to follow my effort of description. We entered the harbour through a maze of channels and ships berthing at a quay down near a railway station. There were a few people on the quay to wave us a welcome, among them being a few soldiers.

The landing of our goods was commenced at once and everyone got busy getting their things together. About 3 p.m. the disembarkation started and we were formed up and marched to a railway station half a mile away. This station was on the outskirts of the town and among the quays, so we did not have an opportunity of seeing any of the lovely views of the city and there was no gay thing to bid us welcome. We were able to get some cakes from some goods-vendors. The carriages, which were to be our quarters for a couple of days, were old narrow and third-class, with only a window in each door, but we managed to make ourselves pretty comfortable. At 5.30 p.m. we moved out of the station. To adequately describe our journey to you I find it utterly impossible, but I shall endeavour to give you an idea of what a Paradise Southern France is.

As stated above we were on the outskirts of the city when we started, and right from the start we passed by pretty orchards, surrounding quaint cottages, which peeped out from great shady trees. On our right terraces rose into the summit of the hills; here and there a large and beautiful residence or chateau stood out prominently from some picturesque position. Below they covered the slopes to the sea and the view we had of these with the harbour and its shipping in the foreground made a delightful picture. Our way led through deep cuttings, long tunnels, embankments and viaducts according to the nature of the hills; the scenery ever-changing, was always of great beauty. We had about four hours to drink in the beauty of the scene before darkness closed down on us. Most of us were too excited to sleep, I think, and it was funny to be in a train again after six weeks on the water.

Daylight showed scenery equal to that which we saw on the previous evening. Picture, if you can, Adelaide hills covered with orchards, vineyards and farm plots, with here and there streams showing like silver threads through the picture! If you can imagine such a scene, you may gain some idea of the exquisite beauty of the whole of the country through which we passed. No one could too highly praise this beautiful country – 'tis a veritable Garden of Eden. The journey was one continual delight and we did not trouble much about rest while we had the opportunity. We gathered round the windows, afraid that if we left them for a moment we would miss some specially beautiful bit, such as a chateau standing proudly out from a beautiful setting of mountains and trees, or a lake glistening amidst the trees and crops, with blue hills showing away back in the distance.

At intervals stoppages were made in order that tea and rations could be served. We lived on iron rations from the time we left the *Afric*[39] until a day or so after landing here. Sometimes we were able to purchase extras, and at one or two places Red Cross ladies served out tea. Those of us who had started learning French tried it on all comers, much to the amusement of all concerned, but sometimes we made our meaning understood. Our officer said the first Frenchman he spoke to in the language nearly fainted!

Some of the most important towns through which we passed were Dijon, Lyons, Versailles and Rouen to Havre – our destination. Of course there were countless other important stations whose names I don't remember, and little wonder when they are spelt in such a funny manner.

Near the end of our trip the railway ran along the banks of France's main waterway, the River Seine. The French people, those in the fields, in the towns, everywhere, were delighted to see us and greeted us heartily. It was hard to realise that in this self-same country, but further north, such a hellish war was

---

39 The *Afric* was the ship that transported Theo to Europe.

being waged. But evidence that all was not as it should be were to be seen everywhere, but in different ways. The scarcity of men was apparent even to us as women were everywhere at work; the fields, munition factories and engineering shops, in close proximity to the railway, had numbers of girls at work, and they turned out to greet us as we passed.

In the yards of these places could be seen munitions of all descriptions. While in one place we saw sections of aeroplanes; on these also the machines were being tested. Trains bearing guns and ammunition were passed. Trains also were taking soldiers on their way to the front and other hospital trains were bringing back the wounded. This was grim reality and made us realise that what we had set out to do was not all a game. At certain places we passed camps of Turkish and German prisoners. At one important centre, the name of which I had better not mention, there were thousands of railway locomotives that had been brought from Belgium, flags flying o'er them and drawn up in close formation. They covered an extensive area.

At Havre, our destination, after being moved around a bit and having partaken of refreshments at a canteen, we moved off to a big military camp a couple of miles distant where we spent Saturday night and Sunday. It was midnight before we got settled down. Sunday was spent wandering round the camp and talking to the Tommies,[40] who told us some gruesome tales of their experiences. No one was allowed out of camp, as usual, so we had a rotten day of it. Early in the evening we marched from the camp to the docks and boarded a fast boat for the crossing of the Channel. The boat did not leave the harbour till pretty late. As all on board had to wear their life belts, all night, you can imagine that little rest was to be had.

I don't know anything about the run across the Channel; I lay amongst a number on deck, and dozed during most of

40 English soldiers

the night, and when awake was too weary to take notice of anything. Daylight found us off the English coast and after a long wait we disembarked. The usual program of standing about for an indefinite period was repeated. At last we boarded a train and set out for Salisbury Plain. It was only a ride of a few hours and I was too tired to notice what the country was like.

At a place called Amesbury we detrained. From here we had a three-mile march, well packed, and it was hard work, for it was a pretty muggy day. Arriving at the camp we had more biscuits and bully beef, and we existed on this tack for a couple of days while our tucker arrangements were being put shipshape.

The date of our arrival in camp was July 24th, so we have been here nearly a fortnight. During that time we have worked hard and route marching is the main thing. There are a couple of nice villages within a 3-mile radius of the camp and during our work we have visited both several times. Their quaint and picturesque houses, with small windows, attic rooms, thatched roofs, etc. are quite a refreshing change for us. These old places look far prettier, in their setting of great trees, shady lanes and hedges, than the modern architecture. Marching in such glorious places as are to be found in these old villages is not work – it's a pleasure. 'Lovers Lanes' are to found everywhere, and finding such bonza places makes me wish that I was able to take my sweetheart for a stroll there. Plenty of places to get lost in, eh, Mill? Streams run through all the villages, it seems, and on two occasions we have enjoyed a swim in a deeper pool at a place called Durrington. It was A.1.

Yesterday we did a 22-mile route march to the city of Salisbury, leaving at 9 o'clock. We arrived just after noon, had only a couple of hours to look around and left for camp again at 2.15, doing the return trip in 3 hours. Only the machine gunners took it on and the 'heads' complimented us on our performance, which was pretty good after only a week's work on the end of six weeks' cramped life shipboard.

We had such a short time in Salisbury that we had only time enough to inspect the Cathedral, which was well worth it. 'Tis a grand old pile, rich in carvings in stone, marble and wood, with grand representations of the disciples and bible subjects. Standing in this wonderful place one could almost feel a 'Presence'. Everything was so calm and still, and the beautiful work that was everywhere in evidence was a source of delight. Many of the carvings are still intact, although hundreds of years have passed since they were wrought. There were tombs of great personages with effigies of knights in armour forming the lids of the coffins; the lids of bishops' coffins had the figure of a bishop wrought in stone. Other carvings in vaults and seats and organ were truly beautiful and wonderful. By the time we had looked over this lovely pile of architecture, it was time to fall in preparatory to returning to Lark Hill camp.

I am sending a parcel by this mail, containing a table-centre affair for Daisy, and a cushion-cover for Mother and Father. In this parcel I will enclose three booklets telling all particulars about the Salisbury Cathedral, one for Mother, another for Ivey and another which I would like you to send on to Mrs. Hastwell.

After a lapse of seven weeks a mail has come to light, but I haven't received all the letters, which I expected. I got a parcel and letter from Mrs. Hastwell, and letters from Bert, Con, Millie, and the two Hastwell girls, Phil and Jude; it was bonza to hear all the news and I will answer them in due course. I was very disappointed not to hear a little bit from all of you, but under the circumstances I must forgive you and hope for more next time. You know a couple of months without any news is a weary old time. I quite expected a letter from Ivey, but none has come to hand. I am sure the dear girl would write, but I suppose the letter has gone astray; so I must grin and bear it.

I believe 3-1/2 tons of letters from S.A. came to hand, so small wonder some have gone astray. I can see that I must not look forward too eagerly for mails, for some boys say they haven't received any letters for months. If I look forward very much, the disappointment will be too keen. I will always write to you all, no matter whether my mail goes astray or not, for I know it will not be the fault of my loved ones if I don't receive them. Still, letters have been trickling in each day, and more may come for me yet, so I won't give up hope.

All troops have a few days furlough on landing here, and tomorrow several of us leave for a look around London, returning on Monday night next. We should have a good time. With the exception of a slight cold, I am as fit as a fiddle. I sent a cable home last weekend and a few days after our arrival I despatched some post cards. I was delighted to hear of the improvement in Fred's condition, and trust the poor old chap will soon be A.1., and that his troubles will end for he has had more than his share of bad luck.

I believe we are to work a different style of gun and will have a lot to learn. Therefore, we may be here for quite a long time yet, so you must not worry about me.

Dearest Mother, it will be your birthday about the time that you receive this, and I trust that it will be a very happy one – nothing is too good for you, dear Mother.

We have to go for pay now, so ta-ta, and fondest love and whips of kisses from,

Ever Your Loving Son and Brother

"Theo" xxxxxxx xxx xxxxxxx

Shaftesbury Hotel
Great St. Andrew Street,
LONDON
August 4th. 1916

My dearest Dad, Mother, Brother and Sisters,
That's a long start, anyway, is it not? Only yesterday I posted a real budget home, but now that I am in this, the greatest city of the world, for a day or two, I must drop you a line from here. Just fancy 'little me' in the vast city of London, strolling around as unconcernedly as if I was back in Mount Gambier! Of course the place is different to what I had imagined, but yet 'tis much the same as any other big town, only everything is on a more stupendous scale: vast crowds, all sorts of vehicles buzzing round, immense buildings – and very wonderful ones, too.

Well, to go back from the beginning:- I told you in the 'budget' that we were coming here today. Leaving Lark Hill Camp this morning we marched to Amesbury and took the train to Waterloo Station, London. The country through which we passed was fine, but not nearly so beautiful as France. Waterloo Station is a whopper with countless people about. From there we marched through various busy thoroughfares to the Australian Headquarters where we had refreshments. A representative of this hotel brought us along here in a bus; after we had spruced up we set out for a look around.

It was about 4 p.m. then. During our rambles we saw many fine buildings, shop windows beautifully dressed and also countless people, girls and womenfolk being very fashionably dressed. The girls over here are not bad, but we decided that they couldn't beat our bonnie Australian girls. Of course we received many smiles and 'glad eyes', so of course we smiled back – that's all. People seem to think a great deal of the Australians over here; even ladies passing in taxi's smiled and waved to us, and the gents also gave us a smile and sometimes a nod, too. Some kids aren't we? That's another indication of the fine reputation 'the boys' have made, eh? And 'tis something for us to keep up when our turn comes! After wandering around a great while, we at last found our way back; after being directed once or twice and after having tea I wandered in here and began to write. As my cough isn't too good I've decided not to go out tonight, but will have a rest instead. I forgot to say that I saw Parliament House, Westminster Abbey and Nelson's Monument at Trafalgar Square (not far from here), so I haven't done too badly, eh? Ta-ta! More anon!

Lark Hill,
Monday

You must excuse this, I've just had an accident with my pen; ink had leaked out into the protector and I didn't know it. [41]

Well, we returned back here between 1 and 2 a.m. this morning, very tired after having to walk three miles from the station. We had a fairly good time but London is not what I expected it to be. It is a very drab-looking place after our sunny land; but of course it is a very wonderful place. The girls are not at all shy – quite the opposite in fact – and we got tired of receiving the 'glad eye'. Some of the styles of dress are a bit peculiar. I cannot give you a decent account of our holiday until next mail, as this one closes almost immediately.

I shall try and get a parcel away by this mail; please give to Ivey the views, etc. which are enclosed; I think it would be best to send all in one parcel. We are all very tired and sleepy today and don't feel like work, but it has to be done all the same.

I believe another mail is close on hand, so I am looking

---

41 Theo is referring to a large trailing blot of ink on the page.

forward to more news and hope not to be disappointed. I am
A.1. again now and trust that all of you are ditto.
Fondest love and kisses from,
Yours Lovingly,
"Theo"

On Active Service
Lark Hill Camp
SALISBURY
August 13, 1916

My dearest Homefolk,
Hurrah, another mail has come to hand and brought me Dad's,
Daisy's and Millie's letters; also two from Ivey, one of which
I should have received last time. It was just lovely to receive
them all.

I am thankful for the inspiration that moved me to write a
letter to you all and to Ivey the day I left. I believe that it did
that which I meant it to; it was easier for us all that I should
write it and not speak my feelings at such a time. Also I thought
it might seem as if I was kind of speaking to you, eh, just when
you were perhaps missing me rather much.

I enjoyed the bit of fun at the Outer Harbour; it was bonnie
to be so close to you and to be able to pass messages. It was
rather tricky though holding on by our toenails where we were.
I remember a tug coming out but there were only two sailors
on her deck and the seas were washing over her, so if that was
the one, you would not be able to see much. I could see you for
a long time from the mast.

I have a cold that is giving me some trouble and which
tended to spoil my days in London, but it's working off. You
bet I'll look after myself as well as I can; I want to keep as fit as

a fiddle. I'll go to Boxley[42] if I can, but I doubt whether I shall be able to get there.

I'm jolly glad that Fred is getting over his bad time; it's about time Fortune smiled on him, poor old chap, don't you think? I hope you are all well and happy now.

Say, Dais, I would like to be able to go with you to meet Mill. Perhaps I will again one of these days. But I guess you will be away on the farm when I come back, eh? Don't forget to tell me the exact date of your wedding, old girl!

Sure I guess Dad's garden did freshen up. I wonder will the lawn be an accomplished fact by the time I land back. I reckoned the censor wouldn't like my small writing. (That was a joke!)

You are right about Ivey, Dais, I know I am the luckiest of kids!

Monday

I say, Mill, you are a dear to write me such bonza long letters. My cold has made me put off my writing until the last minute, so I'll have to again put off answering yours, Bert's and Con's letters until next week and that leaves next Monday I think.

I am sitting in a trench writing this when I ought to be working. I believe we get a beautiful little gun today to start work on, which will be a jolly sight better than messing about as we have been doing since our arrival.

Complaints being made about our tucker, 'the heads' conferred last night; this morning we had porridge, sausages, bread butter and jam – so had a lovely satisfying breakfast.

We had a nice rain during the night and this morning, but now the sun is shining strongly. The rain has made the country fresh and sweet.

By the way, Mother and Dad, I hope you got that extra size

---

42 Boxley was the district from which the Wrights originated

enlargement, like Mill's; be sure and get it if you haven't done so yet.

Au Revoir for the present, dear ones all. Hoping you are all well and happy,

Heaps of love and kisses from,

Yours Lovingly,

"Theo"

Salisbury Plain

Aug.19th, 1916

My dearest Loved Ones,

In my last epistle I promised to tell you a little about my London trip. As I have already in a previous letter told you of the trip up from camp and wrote to you and Ivey on that first night instead of going out, I will start now to tell you what we did from Saturday until Monday.

Always we would start out of a morning from the Shaftesbury Hotel in any direction we fancied, trusting that some time of the night we would find our way back once again. On the Saturday we did not get up until very late; therefore we did not get a start until about dinnertime. In fact that was the case every morning, for we took advantage of a lay-in between the sheets. By the way, it was quite nice to feel bonza clean sheets once again.

However, to get on with the yarn, we went wandering off along some crowded thoroughfares black with hurrying humans and buzzing vehicular traffic, and it was simply marvellous how wonderfully the police controlled this enormous traffic. The London policeman cannot go to sleep on his job – he has to be very much on the alert. He is a very courteous gentleman, too, in spite of the fact that he is continually being asked by people, in all walks of life, to direct them here, there and everywhere. I know the police were a godsend to us soldiers. I know Bert,

Tom and I were indebted to them, for we did not have to go far beyond the hotel before getting lost.

But we would work around in such a way that we would know in what direction our diggings lay, and we would always be somewhere within pretty easy distance of it when we felt like bed. Always a bobby's assistance was sought and we were put on the track. Well, on Saturday we wandered on admiring the many fine buildings, inspecting shop windows, and criticising the styles of some of the fair sex. Some of the girls wore shoes with such high heels with short skirts, which reached very little, if at all, below their knees.

At last we found ourselves in the famous Strand where the crowd was even denser. Later on we passed St. Paul's Cathedral. Dinner at a restaurant cost us 2/6[43.] (The charges at these places were infernally high.)

At a jeweller's shop in the Strand I secured those Machine Gun brooches. A bit further on we entered a show of some kind where one put 1 penny in a slot in a machine, turned a handle and saw moving pictures. A weighing machine scaled me at 11st. 4lb. We also had a shot at a shooting gallery.

Continuing on we came to the Thames Embankment where a crowd was viewing the captured submarine UC5, which you will have read about. All we were allowed to see was her body showing above the water, which gave a view of the conning tower, periscope and mines ready for laying. We remained on and near the Embankment for some time idly watching the crowd there, the boats on the river and, incidentally, having a rest. Had tea, which cost us even more than dinner, 2/9; then went to a picture theatre, where we enjoyed a rest and saw some pretty decent pictures.

---

43 Two shillings and six pence

It was getting on for midnight when we got back to the hotel, and as Bert saw searchlights, we sat on the bed smoking and watching for them to show up again; we eventually turned in without seeing them any more.

Sunday we started out again and went down to Trafalgar Square. From there we went on past the War Office, Admiralty Office and through an entrance where the Horse Guards were mounted on two coal black chargers, in their flash steel helmets, plumes, buff breastplates, with sabres unsheathed and held up and against the shoulder etc. Can you picture them? Passing through here we went on through St. James Park where there were lots of people out for an airing. A keeper told us if we hurried we would see the changing of the guard at Buckingham Palace.

We arrived just in time to see the guard coming away led by a military band flashily uniformed. They and the soldiers looked bonnie, for these 'tommies' are specially put through this ceremonial drill, I believe, and move like clockwork. The palace itself is, of course, a beautiful pile.

Strolling through the park in another direction we went past the Houses of Parliament to the Westminster tube railway station, and travelled by tube to South Kensington, to visit the two museums there. As we got there, a bit before 2 p.m., opening time, we walked around a bit. There are some very nice residences in that part. At the first museum we saw marvellous carved work statues, models of temples and marvellous pieces of carved work from Eastern lands, such as parts of pagodas, carved stairways, etc. Also wonderful models of Japanese bungalows and other pieces of carved work of all kinds. It made me long to be able to carve even the tiniest bit; they were absolutely marvellous in their detail.

In another room were sculptured images and statues of men, women and representations of beasts. Lovely!!!

Yet again there were beautiful tapestries depicting olden

day life and battles; immense and wonderful carpets. Then there was a collection of carved carriages, chariots, etc. As this museum building covered fourteen acres and there were 145 rooms, you will understand that we could not spare the time to see all the wonderful things that it contained.

The second museum, the British Natural History Museum, was some little distance from the first and here were preserved specimens of all kinds of birds, beasts, and insects; also skeletons of the same. There was one elephant in particular which measured 12ft. at the highest part and had tusks 9ft. long. It would take too long to tell you of them all. I must leave you to imagine the varieties of wild and tame beasts in a stuffed state, and skeletons of the same. And there you have the Natural History Museum.

Travelling back to Westminster Station, we went from there to the National Art Gallery. We revelled in the beautiful studies from the brush of Gainsborough, Turner and other artists innumerable. We were informed that the best pictures have been stored in the cellars to preserve them from Zeps;[44] also the roof of the building is sandbagged for the same purpose.

Then we had another tube ride to Richmond, on the Thames, where we mixed with the crowds and watched the numerous boating parties. We had an enjoyable tea in an old garden and arrived home about midnight tired after an enjoyable day.

As only a week has passed since my last letter there is not very much news to relate. On Monday, Tuesday, and Wednesday, the usual routine occupied our time, such as squad drill, bayonet drill, route marching and looking over the Lewis Machine Gun. On Thursday a school of instruction in this gun commenced; four men from each of the four battalions in the brigade were appointed to attend. Bert W.,[45] two other lance

---

44 Zeppelins (large airships) were used by Germany to bomb areas of Europe.

45 Bert Westley

corporals and I represented the 43rd. We are being taught all about the gun and it is mighty interesting work. We have to put in like one thing, for exams are to be held at the end of the course and we may be put on instructing after. This means, both during and after school hours, plenty of swotting.

I'm feeling lovely this week, as 'fit as a hundred fiddles'; it's bonza after the nasty cold I had.

We are expecting to receive a mail about the middle of next week. That will be bonza. I just about know every word in the letters I have received, I do verily believe. I'm longing for a letter from you, Mother darling; I fear that one may have done as the first one did, which Ivey wrote – strayed about! Con said in the first mail that you, Laurie dear, were writing, and it would come by next mail. That also has still to come to light. This mail closes Wednesday next and I may hear from you all before I post this.

Sunday

I wonder have you met my friend, Mrs. Hastwell, yet, Mother dear. I have had so many letters to write, or, at least I've had so much to tell you when I have written, that I don't think I told you of the letter and Prayer Book which I received from Mrs. Hastwell. It was blessed on the altar of St. George's Church, Goodwood, last Palm Sunday, and written on the flyleaf is the following:

Defend, O Lord, this Thy servant with Thy heavenly grace that he may continue Thine for ever and daily increase in Thy Holy Spirit more and more until he come into Thy everlasting Kingdom.

While in the back is the following:

Theo, - with love and every good wish, from his friend Lena Hastwell, Goodwood, Sth. Aus.

In the book Mrs. Hastwell has marked a couple of especially beautiful hymns. 'Tis a bonnie letter. Mrs. H. asked if I had room in my pockets for a little remembrance from her, although she knew I would have tokens of remembrance from all you dear ones to go in those pockets. She said she had read in a paper a sweet little bit about the French women taking one soldier specially and being their godmother, and they pray for that boy specially that God will watch over and protect him. Mrs. H. said she thought it was a lovely idea, so she was going to call herself my godmother and every day I would know she was saying *Our Father* for me.

Don't you think I have made a staunch friend? (I should say friends, for the girls have adopted me as their brother; they said I seemed just like a big brother!) I know that I have the love and prayers of all you dear ones at home, and it is nice too to know that my friends also think I am worthy of their friendship and prayers, don't you think so?

Last night I went to a picture show with Bert and another of our lance corporals, Archie Fletcher, but the programme was not up to standard.

This morning we had to attend a church parade. I consider these precious times wasted for we can never hear what is going on, as there is such a crowd. I would have preferred to be over here writing. Sunday evenings there is always a service, like our own, held in the Y.M.C.A.; they are something decent. Tonight I may go to a service, which one of the chaplains is conducting in the village of Durrington; a number of our boys went last Sunday and enjoyed it immensely. This afternoon I will spend letter writing.

Will leave off now and add more later on – the mail does not close until Wednesday. 'Tis midday here, and I guess over there you are retiring, for it must be 9.30 p.m. by your time.

Monday

I did not go to church last night, but wrote letters instead. I feel quite proud of the fact that I've written one to each of you in addition to this 'home-letter'. When writing yesterday, Mother dear, we half expected that we were off to the front; there was something in the air and all sorts of rumours were flying around. But it has blown over and work is as usual and is likely to continue so.

The N.C.O.s[46] have to attend lectures in the evening now, on top of our work in the school during the day; so you can guess there's plenty to keep us busy. Hurrah! I have been rewarded for sending all those letters and I have received nine altogether from Mother, Con, Ivey, Millie and Laurie. They were all lovely and made me feel very happy. I'm sorry I cannot answer them this time but 'tis impossible.

It was just lovely to receive your beautiful letter, Mother dear, with its many loving passages and kind, sound advice. The letter that I wrote you yesterday, Mother dear, will give an answer to parts of yours. I'm delighted to know your feelings towards Ivey. You know how dearly I love her and what a high opinion I have of her. I guess you and Laurie were lost without each other for so long.

Lights Out is going now so goodnight.

Tuesday

Fred must have been indeed ill, and I am very, very sorry to hear it. But I am delighted to hear that he is getting on well.

I've just heard that the mail I have posted goes via Vancouver and takes a very long time about it. I didn't know that.

About what you mentioned re Strath[47] – I had forgotten all about it and had to think what it was – I.U.A.P!

Au revoir everybody; write heaps of letters - that's all there is to cheer us up.

---

46 Non Commissioned Officers - An enlisted member of the armed forces, such as a corporal, sergeant, or petty officer, appointed to a rank conferring leadership over other enlisted personnel.

47 Strathalbyn – a small South Australian town where Fred, Theo's brother was living.

I'm off to school now!
Heaps of Love from,
Yours,
"Theo"

Lark Hill Camp,
Salisbury Plain
England.

My dearest Homefolk,
On Saturday afternoon last I felt like stretching my legs after a week at the school of instruction, and very little exercise, so Harry Cook and I strolled off to Amesbury and tried to kill time in various ways. There are two villages within the four-mile radius, which is out of bounds when off parade, but our numerous route marches and occasional pleasure walks to them have made their beauty, etc., a bit stale. These villages, although delightfully pretty, are exceedingly sleepy.

So for quite a long time we stayed at the Church of England marquee where we had refreshments and played several games. Tiring of this, we strolled about the village then tried to get served at one of the refreshments rooms, and had to wait three quarters of an hour before we got the boiled eggs which we had ordered, the reason being that the place was crowded with soldiers all clamouring at once to be served. My word the poor girls were rushed off their feet!

After that we went to a passable picture show – then back home. When we arrived there we heartily wished that we had set out for camp earlier; an Australian mail had been distributed and there were four letters for me, and a bill for two pounds and eight shillings from Engelbrecht which had followed me from Morphettville. So I'm glad that I asked you previously to fix it up. It was just lovely to get another mail so soon.

It was getting late when Harry and I lobbed home, and while

I was still deeply interested in reading your letters the bugler sounded lights out and the electric light was switched off. So I was left in the dark and had to quickly put my letters away and scramble into bed, to go off to sleep thinking of 'home' and the dear ones I have left, for a while.

Sunday morning we were hauled off to church parade, but when we arrived at the parade ground the rain just poured down and we dismissed at the double. I spent the remainder of the day reading and writing at the Y.M.C.A. and Church of England huts.

At the school on Monday, besides the usual work we prepared the guns and ammunition, etc., for a day at the ranges on Tuesday. So Tuesday morning we had to turn out at 5.30 a.m., breakfast at 6, and away to meet at a given spot; it was a couple of miles to the ranges.

My word it turned out a horribly dreary day, rained practically all the time and it was also very cold – just a taste of what those already at the front have to put up with. We were mighty glad to get back to the camp and change all our clothes, I can tell you. Next day we had to turn out at the same time as on the previous morning and the weather gave promise of being even worse, however, it brightened up and a lovely day resulted. Somehow or other I did not do well at all in the firing. My shots were just going a bit too high; the chap who was observing for me said I was right on, so I kept at the same elevation; the result was I skimmed the target. Better luck next time!

Sunday 2nd/9/16

On Thursday morning the battalion went for a route march and to spend the day, night and part of Friday digging trenches; we 'school boys' did not go as we had to attend the school that day, and we were mighty pleased, I can tell you. So we had a good time while they were away. It seemed funny Thursday night to be the only ones in the large hut; last night it seemed quite alright to have the rowdy mob back again.

Yesterday we spent our time washing our clothing (of which I had quite a pile), tidying the hut and writing. I hate washing clothes, but as a result of having to do it I'll have plenty of sympathy in future for those who have to do it!

This morning I had my first go (only for a short time) at instructing re the Lewis gun. I think I would like to be given such a position. After that we were taken along to the doctors for another inoculation as a preventative of typhoid; the needle was run in the left arm between the elbow and shoulder this time, and next Saturday we will receive another dose.

There are a couple of good billiard tables in the Y.M.C.A., Dad, where the usual charge is 6d. for half an hour. I have enjoyed several games of late and it helps to pass the time pleasantly.

One afternoon while school was in progress we spotted a lady taking photographs, so one of the chaps hopped out and got her to snap our school. Each of us got half a dozen, so I have sent one on to you Mother and Father; I can't send one to the others for I haven't enough to go round. I'd better not send 'em to any, I s'pose. The photo did not turn out too badly, but of course I am looking serious, as usual.

I am so pleased that Fred benefited by his holiday with you; it was nice for them that you had such a little rain while they were with you. I am sorry to hear that Charlie's fears have been realised. I was not surprised to hear of his trouble, for he told me at Easter that it was what he expected to take place. Fancy Charlie not knowing Fred! But I s'pose it is hardly to be wondered at, considering the circumstances.

Yes, Mother, Laurie did tell me about Mr. Haines being her teacher. I bet Father was wild about that iron being stolen. It seems rather peculiar that it should be lifted after him taking so much trouble to secure it!

Many thanks Mother and Father for the thought re Auntie & Uncle Carr. I want to send them a souvenir when I can find something suitable which also suits my pocket.

When I receive mails from home it seems to me that the 13,000 miles that separates us are bridged. You see, I can picture you all and know just about what you would be doing, and it almost seems as if I have just come by train from somewhere (like I used to from the 'Burg) and you are all telling me what the recent news concerning yourselves is. Do you get my meaning!

Then when I write I try and tell you things in such a way that you too can form some sort of a picture of me in my new surroundings and talk to you about our life here. But when you read those same letters you must not criticise 'em too much, for there is generally a piano going and much talking and laughter where I am writing (although sometimes one is lucky to be in a quiet spot). So if I sometimes get a bit tangled when trying to tell you something you must make allowances and forgive me.

I am surprised that writing paper is so dear. We can get a good supply yet and it is comparatively good stuff; I got fifty envelopes like the one in which the photo postcard is enclosed for two pence, half penny, which was not too bad, I reckon. Most things are pretty dear over here though and we are always thankful when payday arrives.

Do you remember Fred's one-time pal, Alec Kilsby? Well, his brother and young Francis Tormay (Frank Jaiger's nephew) came to my hut to see me the other night, and we had a nice chat. Then another time one of the younger Steele boys came in. It is quite nice to meet these chaps, as you may guess.

The other day I received a letter from France from Len E. McNamara, a lad of 18 or 19 with whom I used to work at the 'Burg. He had just come safely out of one of the hottest engagements of the war. A couple of days previous to writing he received my letter which I wrote in May, not long before we left, and as he had heard that the 43rd were in England he dropped me a line. Of course he could not say much about their doings. He said he would expect a reply within a week and to see that he got it. So I wrote the same night. He also asked if I had a spare photo of myself to send along, for he would like to gaze at my old dial if he could not see me in the flesh. So I sent along one of the small ones which one of the boys took here.

Thank you muchly, Mother dear, but I don't know of anything that you could send me; any odd things that I require I am able to purchase at the Y.M.C.A. and shops here at the camp; if not there at the stores in the adjacent villages. Yes there are even shops here! So you know, every night that I leave the Church of England Hut (which is situated on a rise) and look around, I am vividly reminded of what Adelaide looks like at night, with the electric lights shining through a slight mist – but, of course it is not quite on such a large scale; still I always think of that somehow!

The days are drawing in now, sure enough, and we are getting plenty of rain, which of course means plenty of mud also. A tin of boot polish doesn't last long nowadays.

I think I'll have to keep notes of the letters which I write, for I seem to send away so many that I'm sometimes not quite sure when I wrote last, to whom, and what I wrote about. I think my letters are all a pretty fair length and therefore I spend quite a lot of time writing.

The stuff that was injected into our systems is now well at work on all of us and we all have a mighty stiff and sore 'wing'. It's a funny old feeling I can tell you, and I have to receive two more doses yet. The sooner 'tis over the better – we all hate it!

I believe a mail boat has arrived from Australia, so we are eagerly looking forward to some more bonnie letters, and hoping that we shall receive them before the 6th, the date on which this mail closes.

Mill, 'tis alright to hear the old piano going. Some of the boys who get going on it seem to know all those favourites like the *Norwegian Cradle Song, Rendezvous*, *A Perfect Day*, *Remembrance* and others which you used to play; some of the names of which I have forgotten although I recognise the music, in addition to all the popular topical songs.

One I forgot to mention is the lovely *Long, Long Trail*. It sounds very homelike to hear them. Then usually on Sundays young ladies helping at the Y.M.C.A.[48] play and sing the good old hymns while we are reading and writing, etc. Sure, it's alright!

I can't think of anything more to talk to you about at present so I shall put this epistle away and perhaps there will be more to add in the intervening days before the mail closes.

Monday
4/9/16
I believe the mail closes tomorrow so I must finish this epistle off. I'm afraid the letters are sometimes creased up a trifle, but you must forgive me for I sit down and write as opportunity offers, then I generally have a few tries at folding the paper into shape to get it into the envelope before my efforts are successful.

Hoo-roo! For this time with loving thoughts and heaps of love to each one of you from
Yours lovingly,
Theo.

---

48 Young Men's Christian Association.

Lark Hill Camp
Salisbury Plain
England
10/9/16
My dearest Loved Ones,

It was just lovely to receive all your bonza letters last night –
each one of you chatted to me in first-rate style and after
hearing all you had to say I went quite happily to dreamland.
According to the date of your letters 'tis seven weeks since you
wrote, so you see it takes letters quite a long time to reach us,
doesn't it? Besides your letters I had two from Ivey, one from
Mill, one each from Mrs. Hastwell and Phil and three letters
and a bundle of papers from the Mount.

The mail closes tomorrow, so I haven't the time to reply
minutely to your letters, but hope to do so by the next mail
which I believe leaves somewhere about the 21st. The one
closing tomorrow is I think an extra special one and goes via
Vancouver. I don't know how long it takes to reach you, but I
do know that you, like myself, want all the letters you can get
hold of, so you bet I take advantage of every opportunity that
offers of writing home.

We boys who recently attended the school have this week
been engaged in instructing others. I like the work, and it has
given me a fresh incentive. My detachment, of a little over a
dozen, includes a sergeant and two corporals who of course are
my seniors, but during instruction they are under me. They are
all good fellows, and help me greatly by doing their job and
being very keen on it too. I get on famously with them.

They are so keen that at their request I secured permission
from the O.C. to take a gun over to their hut on Friday evening
so that they could do some more work. They reckoned it was
jolly good of me to take the trouble, but you will see that I
enjoyed it, because I was there from 6.15 to 8.30 p.m. – time

went so quickly. They had the stove in their hut going full blast, so we had buttered toast for supper! After which two men took the gun back to my hut and the sergeant (Lever) and I went for a bit of a stroll and a chat. In the course of conversation he had the kindness to say that 'the men were delighted with their instructor'; he also paid me the compliment of saying that 'he did not think the others could have such a grip of the work as I had'. But of course I would not let that pass; the others can beat me. Anyway such a little bit of praise coming from a member of my detachment, who himself holds the rank of sergeant, helped me lots I can tell you. It makes all the difference when instructing to know that they have confidence in me. My only regret is that I am not such a good shot as I am an instructor on the working mechanism of the gun. But I hope to do well, even at that, later on!

No papers have come to hand, but they always are delivered after the letters. You bet we want the letters first.

So things at home are jogging along alright. That's good. If anything goes awry you mustn't keep it from me, you know; I want to know all that takes place at home. By the way nothing has been said about the special enlargement, which I wanted to be a present from me; I know I did not leave the money to pay for same, but it was to be taken from the allotment money. By the way, I hope you have been receiving that without any trouble.

I'm sorry to hear that the washhouse and contents were distributed round the yard, but 'tis good to know that no further damage resulted. When I heard of the terrific storm that had swept over the city, my first thought was how the house withstood it. Mrs. Hastwell said their balcony was swept from their place; so they were very unfortunate. I'm jolly glad I was not in the tents at Mitcham!!

How are Uncle Bert, Aunty, and the children? Where is their home now? I bet young Jack has grown a big boy now.

Church service was held in the Maple Leaf Cinema this morning; it was quite alright. It seemed more like church in the building and I can tell you, the singing of the hundreds of soldiers sounded great. For several Sundays it has been my intention to go to the village of Durrington to church, but for some reason or other I haven't gone. However I am going tonight. Some of the boys go every Sunday evening.

We have been seven weeks in England doing special training most of the time and this will continue for a few weeks longer. However it is rumoured that we will leave for the front in six or seven week's time. It's about time, too!

I heard yesterday that Leo Sneyd had won the D.C.M.[49] I hope 'tis true; he was a jolly fine clever fellow. His brother, Ern is in this battalion. Also, it was with deep regret that I heard that young Stan Callander, Les Sneyd's pal, had been killed.

Saturday afternoon I had a surprise visit from an old Mount Gambier boy, George Gavens. He is stationed at a camp two or three miles away, and has the rank of sergeant, instructor of physical drill. Of course we had a nice chat about the Mount and various things; it was A.1. to meet him.

Yes, Mother, Frank Browne, Mr. C. G. Browne's son is in the 43rd and George and I went down to his hut on Saturday.

Went to church last night at Durrington – it was alright; I quite enjoyed it.

On returning from church I went across to Sergt. Lever's hut and had a good chat. He won't be in my detachment any more as he leaves this morning for a Divisional School; the two corporals, however, remain. In the Sergt's hut is also an ex-trooper, who was for a long time stationed at the Mount, one named Ern Dunstan. He married one of the Stewarts' girls, and is James' brother-in-law. He gave me a couple of *Chronicles*. I just got back to my hut in time for tattoo roll call and had to finish undressing in the dark.

---

49 Distinguished Conduct Medal

The inoculation has not affected me.

Enclosed you will find rather a beautiful little rural scene which one of our boys snapped; it's only a couple of miles from here and a sample of a typical English scene.

General French will inspect us tomorrow; I hope he will be satisfied with the look of us.

I must go now; I'm pretty busy nowadays.

Above all, don't forget you are not to worry; I have no fears whatever as to the future and I'm quite happy and in excellent fettle. So *Au Revoir*; guess I will write again next week end and will try and write a separate letter for each one. I hope you will always have time, each of you, to write me a letter.

Fondest love to all, and with it the hope that you all continue to be in good health.

Lovingly Yours,
"Theo"

Lark Hill Camp,
Salisbury Plain,
England
16/9/16

My dearest Mother, Father, Sisters and Brother

Quite a long start isn't it? But I'm afraid the letter won't be the same for I have very little news to relate this time, as my time has been spent in instructional work. Bert and I were just saying we will have to stir ourselves up and go about a bit in the effort to rake up some news. One day is about the same as another now.

We are beginning to realise what a winter in this part of the world will be like. During the past week we have had exceptionally cold nights and mornings and a couple of days the cold conditions continued all day. Our bunks, however, keep us bonza and warm, and at night I am usually curled up snugly and on the way to the Land of Nod before lights out. But it hurts to have to turn out when 'Reveille' goes at 6 a.m., when we have only half an hour to dress, wash, etc., fold our blankets and stack our bunks. You bet we stay under cover for a few minutes after time if we possibly can – until someone pulls the blankets off! The cold air does the rest! It doesn't take long then to jump into one's clothes, I can tell you.

Those doing physical jerks are alright, but we four instructors have to take a dozen men each from 6.30 to 7.30 and sit down by the gun and tell 'em all about it. A mighty cold job, as you will no doubt agree. I really don't mind it, however, for I like the job.

So far no promotions have occurred, but we hope to get a rise soon. The job would be more acceptable if we had the pay that should go with it. But all things come to those who wait – if they wait long enough, eh?

Who do you think paid us a visit during the week? No less a personage than General French.[50] He came around the camps inspecting the Australians at work – and there are quite a number of troops from the 'Land of the Southern Cross' here, I can tell you. This morning orders contained a report of his verdict. He wished the men to know that he was very pleased with the efficiency shown by the various units, and was impressed by the fine physique of the men and said they would be a valuable contribution to those at the front. He and his large cavalcade of staff and other officers passed us while we were going into action with the guns. All the Lewis gunners of the 11th Brigade work on the one parade ground and they were hard at it, so you

50 General French had a long military career. At this time he was serving as Commander of the British Home Forces from 1915-18.

can guess there was quite a number going their hardest. Would you not like to see us at work? I bet you would! And I wish you could pay us a visit.

One dinner hour we were called out for a special parade and only had a short time for dinner and then to tumble into uniforms (work is usually done in dungarees for the gunners have to lay down in all kinds of places). On being formed up on the parade ground we found that some 'big gun' of the Salvation Army was going to 'open fire' on us. Only a small proportion of the chaps could hear what was said – he got wound up and held forth on the same old subject – 'The various temptations that a soldier runs up against'. We are always having this dinned into our ears and get mighty sick of it.

Yesterday all the Lewis gunners of our division went for a route march for about three hours, passing through one of the pretty adjoining villages on the way (Amesbury). We passed also the historical pile of Stonehenge, which we can see across the plain from this camp; of which I had previously told you.

You remember Longfellow's *Village Blacksmith*, well the 'spreading chestnut tree' and smithy are in a village not so very far away. I have not yet visited the place, but I must do so; Bert went there some time ago.

Fancy Auntie Else being tied up at last, it can't really be true. No I don't know the chap in question!

I am glad you met Mrs. Hastwell, Mother dear, and I hope you took a liking to each other, I think you would. Yes, they have had bad luck, too. Mr. Hastwell over on the West Coast for his health, and during his absence to have their balcony blown down!

I'm mighty glad that Opie's[51] have left the shop and gone to East Adelaide to live. Ivey will be nearer my loved ones now,

---

51 The parents of Ivey Opie, Theo's fiancée.

eh? I'm mighty glad she was able to go to Strath., while Mill was there; Ivey told me what a bonnie time she had.

You see I'm answering your letters and forgot to say that while I was commencing my pleasant weekend pastime of writing home, Bert came to the Church of England hut where I was and handed me half a dozen letters, which I was just delighted to receive. So far we have been exceedingly lucky in getting our letters – long may it be so!

I'm mighty pleased you got my cable alright. Perhaps the length of time taken for it to get to you can be explained by the fact that special rates are allowed to soldiers, but they don't guarantee prompt sending of cable. If it wasn't for these rates I'm afraid to cable home would be out of the question for some of us. Sure, you heard the news of our arrival from quite a number of folk, didn't you?

Life and I are getting along famously, Mother dear (I have no complaints).

Our camp here beats the Australian camps all to bits. But of course the huts were made so comfortable because of the long cold winter months. Our bed consists of low trestles about six inches high on which are placed three long wide boards. On top of that goes a straw-filled mattress and we have also a straw-filled pillow; last of all three blankets and a rubber sheet. Not half bad, eh? Yes our boys are well looked after and are very healthy.

It was so very good of you, dear ones, to make up a parcel for me and I am looking forward to Capt. Stewart's arrival – not only to receive the parcels, but also to see him and enjoy a chat. Ivey is a dear kid to send me one too!

I am rather curious as to what the Blundens[52] are like.

---

52 Cousins related to Great Aunt Jane Blunden – Alice's foster mother. When the Wright family moved to Bakewell Street Evandale, Aunt Jane came to live with them as Alice would inherit from Aunt Jane.

Mother, dear, I wish you wouldn't work so jolly hard. Can't you manage to ease up sometimes, just to please me?

It is good news to hear that Dad is better and I do hope you will continue to be in good health, Dad. It's just rotten to be off colour, isn't it? It is good to know that you still have some work coming in, and I hope you will secure enough to keep you going.

I was hoping to hear from Prospect, but there's nothin' doing. Glad they are A.1., but I was sorry to hear that Cons has been unwell for so long; after two months of it, it was quite time she began to mend.

Sure, I won't know the gardens when I come back. I hope your labours will be bountifully rewarded, Mother and Dad, dears.

Bert[53] and I swap letters (except my love letter); he likes to hear all your news too.

I do wish I was home for October 11, but I'll pay Daisy a visit when I get back to make up.

I appreciated your loving message at the close of your letter, Mother dear.

Heaps of love to one and all,
Yours very lovingly,
"Theo"

Lark Hill Camp,
Salisbury Plain,
England
2/10/16

Dearest Homefolks,
In my last letter I referred to our intended week of practising trench warfare in trenches some distance away on the plain. So

---

53 Bert Westley

now I will try and give you some idea of our experiences on that occasion.

On the Monday morning in question it was horribly wet so the 'heads' decided to postpone the move until the weather cleared up. In the afternoon as the rain had disappeared the battalion set off out of camp and joined up with the other three battalions of the 11th Brigade. Each man had his full pack up, also rifle; our blankets and the Lewis guns were conveyed by transport. A wide detour was made round Stonehenge and we were treated to a few hours solid marching before we came within sight of the trenches, when it was getting dusk.

Of course, the column of troops looked to me a great size. You know what one battalion looks like on the march, well, multiply that by four and you will get a good idea of the number of soldiers engaged.

On arrival at our destination the troops soon settled down in picturesque groups, with some woods as a background, resting and waiting for tea. We were fortunate in getting bread, salmon and onions, so did fairly well.

The country around here is, I think, wrongly called a plain – it is all hill and dale, with occasionally villages of various sizes settling snugly in a valley. All seem to have beautiful trees and a stream or two running through them. We were not given a very long rest for soon after tea we were assigned our positions in the trenches, each of us three lance-corps. and Bert. W. taking charge of a gun and team. We wended our way through various communication trenches to the front trench, at each flank of which two guns with their attendant teams were posted. Arch Fletcher and I were placed at the left flank and took turns at taking charge of the men and guns, having eight hours on and the same time off. It was pretty cold for us beginners, especially on the first night when I couldn't sleep, no matter how I tried during my few hours off.

Each morning between the hours of 5 and 6 o'clock all

hands – and the cook – had to 'stand to arms' ready to withstand any attack that the enemy should make, for you know just before the dawn is, and always has been, a favourite time for launching an attack. So it fell to my lot on the first morning to wake up my chaps, and they did not appreciate my endeavours one little bit, I assure you. They did not relish being called at that hour just to stand about in the cold. Had it been a real attack I guess they would have turned out quickly enough! They cheered up, however, a bit, when later on they saw the mess orderlies making an appearance with breakfast.

But soon the cooks were called all sorts of uncomplimentary names, for the soup they sent out to us was abominable stuff. It tasted just as if some fat had been stirred up in hot water! Can you taste it? Ugh! It made my tummy complain all day. Still it was not the cooks' fault, I guess, for they had to make the best of what they could get. That was our only cause of complaint with regard to the food; we had plenty of bread and jam, cheese, etc., afterwards.

Some of us had taken possession of small dugouts, which had been constructed by the former occupants. So after breakfast I set to work to enlarge it and after a fair bit of labour managed to construct a snug little burrow large enough for two. It was a bit too snug for I hated having to crawl out to take my turn on duty. Each day the gun teams had some time out of the trenches for a rest and to clean up the guns – also to indulge in a much-needed wash if there was sufficient water available.

Then at dusk we would return for another night's vigil, which would often be broken by an alarm to stand by to defend our positions, or to vacate trenches that were being too heavily shelled by the enemy; or, again, to use gas masks to frustrate a gas attack. All being imaginary attacks, of course! We were supposed to act just as we should do if we were actually doing the real thing; of course that is a very hard thing to do, as you will agree.

When the star shells were fired, 'No man's land' would be brilliantly lit up and we were instructed how to place ourselves when out in the open, so as to make ourselves practically indistinguishable, when the enemy sent up star shells to see what we were up to.

On the Wednesday night a grand attack was made on the enemy's trenches, our troops advancing in four separate waves, each wave having a Lewis gun on their flank. It was my luck to be with the last wave and, of course, in a dinkum go wouldn't have seen much of the mix. The waves surged out of our fire trenches in succession and took up their positions as previously arranged. It was pitch dark and mighty hard to keep in touch with each other. Another battalion was acting as the enemy; therefore, each side was on the lookout for prisoners. Although my team lost touch of the wave for a few minutes we were not molested and soon caught up again. We had a dull time, lying out in the cold damp grass for a long time, and were not sorry when the engagement ended.

As we could not use the ordinary blank ammunition in the guns, we scraped together a tin with a stone inside. We used it to indicate our machine gun fire, by rattling the tin and making as much noise with it as possible – a very poor substitute indeed.

The operations lasted for a few hours, ending after midnight, and then it was my turn to take charge. I secured a couple of buckets of coffee for my chaps, and my word it was delightfully refreshing. After having that I didn't want to stay on guard, so I gave my watch to the man then on duty at the gun, and told him to call the reliefs in turn. Then I rolled up in my blankets and enjoyed a couple of hours sleep.

Thursday morning the Lewis gunners moved out of the trenches and encamped under canvas in the rear. We continued to train gun teams and spent the time 'til Saturday very pleasantly in this way, for the weather during the latter part of the week, was delightful.

On leaving the trenches we carried with us, on our equipment and persons, ample evidence of the chalky nature of the ground where the trenches were dug. We were real white men. This, of course, meant more work in cleaning up, and the guns also used to get in an awful mess. We always seemed to be cleaning up something. Before I switch off on to something else, I will tell you of some rather funny acts in regard to our experiences in the trenches.

During the Wednesday night's attack a couple of men passed in front of where a couple of our guns were posted. Our G.C. told them they could not pass that way as a couple of machine guns were trained on them. One replied, 'I don't care a damn if you've got ten howitzers trained on me'. Our little sergeant secured a prisoner whom he took up before the officer and commenced rather a long yarn as to how he had made the capture. While he was thus engaged the captive 'ducked', much to the amusement of our chaps who have no love for this cocky little fellow.

One man carrying the spare parts wallet belonging to one of the guns fell headlong into a trench; and later on Bert W. did likewise. Early next morning one man guarding a Lewis gun had his head too high above the parapet. When accosted by an officer who asked what he was doing up there, the chap, who is a bit of a wag, replied, 'Oh, I'm just getting an eyeful of the daybreak'. The officer was too surprised to reprimand him, I believe.

Yesterday week (Sunday), Bert and I started off for a stroll, heading for Durrington; the afternoon was a beautiful one and we agreed that a walk would do us good. In the beautifully fresh air and sunshine the lovely spots in this sleepy village appeared to acquire additional beauty. We each carried our writing materials with us and on reaching the bank of a stream, in a particularly charming spot, sat down with the intention of doing some writing. However my good intentions in that direction did not bear fruit, I preferred to lie there and dream. Soon clouds obscured the sun and the old earth changed to its usual old drab colour, so I proposed that we continue walking, and pay a visit to Figheldean, where stands the chestnut tree and village smithy made famous in Longfellow's poem, you know the one:

Under a spreading chestnut tree
The village smithy stands ...

The boughs of the giant chestnut tree almost hide the smithy and I secured one or two leaves to send home as souvenirs, also some holly leaves from the church opposite. The leaves that I secured are not very nice specimens; military police are posted at the tree for the purpose of protecting it as soldiers in search of leaves damaged it a bit. We had a look around the ancient church and then strolled along to a place where tea was in progress and had some refreshments. Afterwards we wandered round the village for a short time and then set out for camp.

We made a short cut through someone's private property, where there were beautiful trees, grass and a lovely stream. We crossed the stream at dusk, and had to stand on the plank bridge for a time and take in the beauty of the scene. Trees overhung the stream, also reeds from which twittering waterfowl emerged, one by one, to swim and feed along the stream; then the placid surface would be disturbed by a fish leaping from the water and falling back with a splash. It was beautifully peaceful and quiet there and we stood there for a long time enjoying our surroundings, only making a remark to each other now and again. We soon had to move on, however, for it was getting dark and we had to hurry back to camp.

The following day, Monday, the 11th Brigade held a sports meeting in the afternoon, the grounds being about a mile away. Each of the 4 battalions marched to the sports ground, where their representatives competed in several pedestrian events and foot races of various distances: hurdle races, tug-o'-war, long jump, high jump, etc. Many good finishes resulted with the contestants sometimes having to put up with some good-natured chaff from the interested spectators.

One of the funniest events was the mule race. About half dozen of these stubborn beggars ran the distance several times with different riders on. One was a tartar, and several riders were thrown and tossed about before one chap managed to stick on. Another mule, every time he ran, would run inside the ropes and scatter the boys in all directions, doing the same thing with each rider. No matter how the chaps whipped up their steeds they would not increase their slow clumsy gallop. I bet some of the boys would not be able to sit down comfortably next day, for they rode their steeds bare backed. The Colonel yelled out to one boy to keep his mule off the foot running track, and the lad replied laughingly, 'Lor' blimey, he goes where he likes'. That, I think, describes a mule pretty well.

At about 8 o'clock on last Wednesday morning, had you been anywhere in this vicinity, you would have seen columns of troops and artillery all making for one point – Bulford – which is about three or four miles from here. All these troops, artillery, infantry and all, were Australians. They were all congregating to be reviewed by the King, and as there was between 35,000 and 40,000, you will realise what an imposing sight they made, especially when formed up in review order. Everywhere one looked troops were drawn up and there were so many that the time disappeared; away in the distance on another flank the artillery batteries were barely visible.

Each battalion has its brass band and on this occasion the bands were massed together, and we were treated to some music. As His Majesty and retinue came up a blast was blown on the bugle, and the assembled troops gave the 'royal salute' while the massed bands played the National Anthem. The King passed along the whole length of the lines, after which the whole division marched past the saluting base where His

Majesty and his following were standing. It was a grand sight, indeed, although of course those taking part in it could only get a partial view of the ceremony. Platoon after platoon came along in what appeared to be an endless stream. Each platoon casting head and eyes to the right and the officer in charge saluting as they passed His Majesty. Each platoon vied with the other in the effort to keep shoulder to shoulder and have an absolutely straight line, so that the march past was very good.

I neglected to mention that the march past was headed by several batteries of artillery, who presented a brave sight as they moved along, keeping their high-spirited horses in order and keeping their guns and limbers in an almost unbroken line. After passing the base the battalions formed up one behind the other in a solid mass and when the King passed, on his departure, hats were waved frenziedly on the muzzles of rifles, the sight presenting a resemblance to a vast forest that is being disturbed by a strong wind.

After the King had left the troops moved off in a succession of battalions, and the boys were glad that it was over; nothing is more wearying than to stand for long periods doing a waiting game. We got more of that than we cared for that day.

While awaiting the arrival of the King we were greatly interested in the gyrations of an aeroplane. The aviator, evidently thinking that he had a mighty good opportunity of showing his prowess to such a mighty throng, did some things that left one breathless. He would go at full speed and turn 'til his plane was right on its side. Then would come a series of dives, twists and turns, which made the onlooker expect, all the time, to see man and machine come crashing to earth. But that was not the best he could do, for he finished up 'looping the loop' several times in succession, after which he made off at top speed and was soon lost to sight.

On Thursday and Friday we put through our teams of Lewis gunners whom we have been training in their classification firing; we four instructors also did some shooting. On the first day I got 'good, very good, and good' for three practices, and on the second day I shot pretty well and scored ten points short of the possible, getting 70 out of a possible 80. So you can imagine how pleased I am. I have not been satisfied or quite happy since I made a mess of it last time. I can't account for that – perhaps I worried too much over it. Anyway, I'm a first class gunner now. All the teams did well, most of them securing a 1st class, and several managing the possible – 80 points. We had some of the crack shots of the battalion in our teams. We instructors were of course delighted at the result of the shoot. Friday it was a miserable day, for it rained most of the day; rotten for shooting.

Saturday was a holiday, for on that day a big program of sports was carried out by the 3rd Division. Bert and I had leave to go to London and we left Amesbury, in company with another chap from our section at about 1 p.m., arriving in the city soon after 3. We bustled about looking for a bed for the night and after some going from one place to another we got a bed at a temperance hotel. After tea we started out in the direction of the Strand and making enquiries to set off to see the Zepp relics on view somewhere or other; I couldn't tell you the name of the place even now.

When we arrived at the exhibition we saw a long line of people slowly moving in a few at a time. We began to speculate as to how long it would take for us to get there; but the 'Bobbies', observed our uniforms and then took us to the head of the procession and piloted us in. Some boys, eh! It was something to see the relics, even though they did present a veritable scrap heap of twisted wire, broken sheets of aluminium and damaged parts, which preserved some semblance of their correct shape. It was all interesting but would not give one any idea of the Zepp as it looked in all its mighty power before its destruction.

After seeing all that was to be seen here we set off back

to the Strand where we had tea at some 'restaurant de luxe'. Sure, it was stylish – everything up to the knocker and a lovely orchestra playing part of the time; the *Long, Long Trail*[54] was especially appealing to us! For all its style we did not have to pay so much as we did at some places on our last visit. Having enjoyed a nice rest here we started off in search of some place where we could spend the evening and hit on a picture show where a long film depicting the actual fighting at the front was shown. These took up most of the program and showed parts of the Battle on the Somme in all its awful detail. I won't attempt to describe it, even if I felt I could do the thing justice, I would not try. Although often it made one catch his breath, it absorbed my whole attention, for it showed what we will very likely be experiencing before long.

On Sunday we wandered round very much as we did on the previous occasion, finding our way to most of those places which we visited before. We caught the 9.42 p.m. train home, and just as we were making for our train policemen were flying around seeing that all prominent lights were extinguished as Zepps were over London. Our train moved out of the city at a snail's pace and kept up its crawl until we were well on our journey. Bert and I were in the guard's van packed in with other soldiers until we could hardly move. I had to stand all the way home and then had to walk the three miles from station to camp, turning in about 2 a.m. and up again at 6.

We have taken over another batch to train as Lewis gunners. I can assure you we are kept very busy.

I think I've written a pretty good letter this time. Am anxiously awaiting another mail, which seems long over due. I'm in the pink of condition and good health.

I was terribly shocked to hear that my 'Burg pal, Hurtle Walker was killed last month, and another, Alf Moore, had his

---

54 A popular song at the time.

leg blown off. This is an awful ending to my letter, but war is no respecter of persons is it, and Hurtle has been in it from the outset.

Au Revoir, dearest ones, with best and fondest love from Your loving son and brother,
"Theo"

Lark Hill Camp
Salisbury Plain
England
8/10/16
My dear Loved Ones,

It is only a few days since I sent my last mail, but as there is another closing to-morrow, to go via San Francisco, I must send one by it, for I guess you will like all it is possible to get.

Wednesday was a red-letter day for us, combining the two best things – 'mail day' and 'pay day'. We had been expecting a mail for some days and were beginning to wonder when it would come or if something had happened to it. But at last it arrived and brought a dozen letters for me, much to my delight.

After tea I took my budget over to the Church of England hut and was soon buried in my correspondence from loved ones, sweetheart and friends – all lovely letters, speaking of home, dear ones and friends, telling how things were going on over the seas.

Both Phil and Dorothy H. told of the violet farm, and Ivey wished she could show me how lovely the hills were looking. Phil wrote from Clarendon where she was spending a holiday and painted quite a nice little pen picture of how bonnie the hills were looking, clothed in their spring garb, with wattle out in bloom; she enclosed a sprig, which pressed well, and kept its colour. So I am able now to carry a little bit of Australia with me in my pocket, as well as sundry other flowers which have been enclosed by different ones. After reading my letters I sat back in my chair and had a comfy smoke – you can guess where my thoughts were!

I received Mill's letter dated August 18th at the same time as those from you all written about the 22nd. Yes, Mother dear, I'm glad I have staunch friends! You mustn't take notice of all the rumours you may hear, few of them are founded on fact, and most are twisted and added to until they have no semblance to the original tale. Incredible rumours get going here, and we have learned to take notice of only those tidings that come from the right quarter. 'Tis the first I've heard about the atrocities you mentioned re diseased germs and rats. I am indeed sorry to hear of the misfortunes that have befallen those boys you mentioned. I bet there are lots of boys over here whom I know, both in hospital and in the different camps, but 'tis unlikely that I shall meet them. I bet Daisy and Ted had a bonza time together – lucky kids! I also received a letter from Fred; it's bonza to know that things are going well with them.

'Tis bonza to hear that Dad is being run after, as his work would speak for itself and be the best advertisement. I hope things will boom, but I hope he won't work too hard. So I suppose Dad is at Willunga now – that would be a change of scene for him, too. I do hope, Dad, that you won't let work get you down and worry you!

Mother, dear, don't you work too hard either, I don't like to hear that your arm is troubling you. I want to find you all quite well and happy when I come home, you know. But you always were a battler. I do hope you will ease off and rest as much as possible. Surely you don't believe I would get tired of reading my Mother's letter do you? But I know it was only a joke!

I don't know where Harold Daenke[55] is, so I can't give him your message; I haven't seen him since we left the old *Afric*.

---

55 Harold Daenke was brother to Fred Daenke, brother-in-law to Theo.

I guess the girls would like me to write them each a letter, so I will try and do so. The mail leaves tomorrow and something may turn up to prevent me writing – one never knows – if so, I shall have a letter ready for them for next mail.

My thoughts are with you, especially today. How excited you will all be at the approval of the wedding. I can see you all around the tea table at home, with Bert and Ron and the 'pigeon pair'[56], also Ted, I guess, and perhaps Ivey. What a gay party! The birds in the 'nest' are gradually getting fewer, Mother and Dad, aren't they; the oldest ones are all very happy and I'm sure Daisy will be also. Even this nestling, who has gone for a flight across the seas for a short while, is happy too, and is always with you in spirit even tho' he is thousands of miles away. So don't you worry about me, any of you. I'm A.1. in all respects, in the best of health and quite happy.

With the very best and fondest love and heaps of kisses,

From,
Your loving son and brother,
"Theo"

P.S. – I gave up writing a diary long ago. 'Tis unnecessary, for I tell you all the news in my letters, and to put down everyday doings would make poor reading, you know. I'm enclosing the leaf from the Chestnut tree, which was the theme of Longfellow's poem, also, a holly leaf from a little ancient church opposite. T.W.

… [57]Next day the battalion went out on a field-firing scheme. Our O.C. wanted the Lewis guns so that our section could practice with them. As we could not carry on instructing

---

56 Theo's sister Daisy is soon to marry Edwin Slater – 11/10/16

57 Page 1 of this letter is missing.

without the guns, we instructors had to go also. The battalion is always going out on long route marches, or some scheme or other, lately; but we instructors and those whom we have been instructing have been exempt. The march to the field of operations was a long one and made me pretty tired. We got there about dinnertime after being about three hours on the way. After dining sumptuously on a couple of pieces of bread and jam, work was begun.

Automatic targets would appear at various ranges at intervals and we had to pepper them while they remained in view. It was good practice and our boys did pretty well, scoring several hits every time. Our targets were tiles, resembling the heads of Germans appearing above the trenches; had they been real Germans they would have experienced a pretty hot time.

Not far from where we were firing was a big flying school and late in the afternoon the 'birds' began to make their appearance. Quite a flock of them engaged in all sorts of aerial manoeuvres and it was a bonza sight, for there were several types of them. One fellow was a daisy and did all sorts of daring feats, like the aviator performed on the day we were reviewed by His Majesty – probably he was the same chap; the machine was the same type. He turned, twisted, dived and looped the loop so swiftly just like a blessed swallow. It was lovely to see him – it was a great sight to see them all!

We didn't get home till late that night and after tea. The guns had to be thoroughly overhauled, so we had an extra heavy day's work.

Friday was spent instructing. On Friday night the battalion went out on an all-night stunt, leaving about 10.30 p.m. and arriving back looking utterly weary about 8 a.m. We instructors did not have to go and were allowed to sleep in by our O.C. who took charge of the early morning parade. Good of him, wasn't it?

Yesterday morning it was pretty fine so we gave our teams

gun drill most of the time. It was alright, too, altho' I got pretty hoarse from shouting orders, trying to make my orders heard against the force of a strong wind. I love the work and am making good progress; our O.C. is a bonza old chap and helps us all he can!

Yesterday afternoon I did a bit of washing and writing. Last night the electric light failed for some time and that interfered with my correspondence.

This morning I pottered around fixing up my things and having a general clean up. We did not have to attend church parade, as our boss wanted us to overhaul the spare parts of the guns and tools, etc. Most of the boys are writing home. You should be getting letters pretty frequently now for I seem to be always writing letters. Now I will answer queries, etc., as well as I can.

Fancy, Wednesday will be the 11th – Daisy's wedding day – and I won't be able to participate in the joyous event!! Never mind. I would like to send a cable, only I'm financial enough.

Thanks so much for your loving letter Mother, Millie and Laurie. The *Chronicle* came to hand yesterday, and it was A.1. to be able to read about the doings in Australia. There seems to be a great deal of agitation re conscription. I don't wish to see it, and the majority of the soldiers I've heard discussing it, feel likewise about the matter

Lark Hill Camp,
Salisbury Plain,
England
15/10/16
My dearest Loved ones,

Capt. Stewart paid the officers of the 43rd a visit on Thursday – he knows all of our officers he says – and brought with him the parcels from you and from Ivey. Mr. Osborne, our O.C., brought the news of his arrival to me just as we were preparing to leave the parade ground to go to dinner; he said he had left a parcel in the office for me, brought by Capt. Stewart. Was I excited? Sure! I rained a few questions on the O.C. and learned that Mr. Stewart was a guest at headquarters and would be in camp until evening. Of course I wanted to know when I could see him, and he said it would be best to go along after officers' mess. I arrived at the hut and it was not long before I had stripped off the wrappings and brought to light all the goodies packed by loving hands far across the sea, giving ample evidence of their kind thoughtfulness. How very good of you all, and I thank you so very, very much. Could you but see my pleasure, you would have had ample evidence of my delight. I soon sampled the dates and preserved ginger and so did some of my pals, and oh, they were delicious. You and Ivey didn't forget my fondness for preserved ginger – and I soon found that my mates had a 'sweet tooth' for it also.

The books were well chosen; the only one I happened to have read is *We Two*, but the books will go the rounds of the hut and we all highly appreciate them. On several occasions I have been on the point of buying a book and have got a couple since being here. It is lovely to have a good book to read. I have finished *The Handicap* and liked it immensely. Now I'm interested in *In Deadly Peril*, while a couple of the other boys are deeply engrossed in the others. So you see, your gifts do not give pleasure to myself alone.

The tinned goods are being kept in hand until we go into the trenches; they can be easily packed away in my pack and will make us happy later on. The 'baccy' hasn't been tried yet; I believe it's a wee bit strong. Capstan medium is a smoke I like. The brand, which Ivey sent, is nice and mild, too.

I say, we had some fun over *The Minx by Spoonlight*. We were a long time trying to piece the puzzle, even with about half a dozen lending a hand. Often we were quite certain that some pieces had strayed, when one of us would pounce on a piece that fitted. At last the picture was complete and we envied the 'spooners' you bet.

The Corp. received his share and doubtless is writing to thank you. Once again, please, each one of you accept, from the bottom of my heart, my most sincere thanks for the goodies you sent me – it was so very good of you.

After dinner Bert and I went up to the officers' mess to see Capt. Stewart. Mr. Osborne was keeping a lookout for me and he went in to bring the Captain out. It was A.1. to meet him and have a chat about those at home and the trip across. We spent a happy quarter of an hour or so, when I had to reluctantly say goodbye and get ready for the afternoon parade.

Yesterday afternoon Vern Dunn strolled into our dining room just as I had finished dinner. I wasn't surprised to see him, for one of the chaps in my squad had been to this particular camp the night before and Vern had asked about me, and, of course, I was told about it. As it was a good afternoon for a walk with a rising wind to blow away the cobwebs, we set out for Durrington and had a good old yarn about the good old times at the Mount. Returning to camp we had tea at the C.E. hut and then spent the evening at one of the picture houses. Meeting Capt. Stewart and also Vern this week, has made it a happy one for me. Speaking about the folks at home and the old associations seems to bring the homeland nearer. You understand! The visit of these two is the only thing of interest that I have to relate this time.

Tomorrow week we four expect to go for four days leave and I am wondering what sort of a time I will have at Calne.[58] If Ivey's relatives are as nice as Opie's then, I shall have a happy holiday.

---

58 Market town in Wiltshire, South West of England.

Bert and I go through a bayonet fighting course on our return; the other two attend one during this week.

More anon! xx – xx. T.

Monday 16/10/16

Last night another chap and I started out from here with the intention to attend the church service at Durrington, but it was too late to do so. So we spent a short time having refreshments at a soldiers' tent, after which we strolled round the village and then set out back to camp. The others had some cocoa made, so we made toast and had a good time. Some style, eh! But it tasted lovely and we were very comfortable, I can tell you.

During the day we carry on with our usual work.

Today and tomorrow are voting days for us, when we give our verdict regarding conscription. I haven't voted yet; I said previously that I was not in favour, but after reading the question up a bit and hearing different views I am rather inclined to vote for it, believing it to be in the country's best interests. The authorities seem to be wanting to get hold of the 'slackers', not the married men and those who are exempt, as their duty lies at home. It's a big question and requires careful handling by those in authority.

We expect a mail on Wed., the same day that this one closes; isn't it a pity that we can't receive letters so that we can reply by return. My news is at an end, so *Au Revoir* for this time.

With lots of love and kisses to each one of you, from, Yours lovingly,
"Theo"

P.S. Letters have arrived - a day sooner than we expected 'em. Hurrah! You bet I'm a happy kid. I am so <u>very</u>, <u>very</u> glad to hear that things are running more smoothly. They were beautiful letters from each one of you. To be sure, I was with you in spirit on the 11th. The weather is wet and beastly cold! I am always busy either writing or something to do with the instructional work – have to go through physical jerks and bayonet fighting in a few days time; two of the instructors are in a school now and Bert and I go in the next one. I'm hoping that it won't interfere with our few days leave. As you will know by now I always receive the letters alright and the papers fairly regularly; this time letters from Dad (from Willunga), Mother, Bert, Fred, Dais, Mill and Laurie; also from 'my sweetheart', Phil and Mrs. H. and two papers. Thanks so much dear ones. I am in finest fettle[59] and always hungry – good sign, eh?

My woollen articles don't seem to wear, Mother, dear. As regards other clothes, they are pretty fair, thanks, and I will be fixed up alright, I believe, before we go to the front.

I have to go on parade now, so *Au Revoir*!! xx – xxx – xxx – xxx – xxx – xxx – xxx - xxx
Best of love – "Theo"

Lark Hill Camp,
Salisbury Plain,
<u>England</u>
17/10/16
My dear Dad,

That was a lovely letter that I received today, and I was overjoyed to hear that you were getting on so well at Willunga.[60] I do hope that for you the tide has turned and your worries and troubles will be ended. It is a nice time of the year to be working in the hills – springtime, eh! I can picture how lovely the hills are looking and can see you at work. It would be great if Mother

---

59 Proper or sound condition

60 Theo's father, Joseph Wright was a carpenter/builder. As travelling was done by horse Joseph often had to live on site, away from the family home.

and the girls could spend a weekend with you; they would enjoy that immensely, I am sure.

I am in the best of health, Dad, *as fit as a fiddle* as the saying goes. The life agrees with me and I am getting on A.1. with the instructional work on the Lewis machine gun. On Thursday, Friday and Saturday next, those who are now finishing their 3 weeks course will be put through their firing test at the ranges. I have hopes of most of those in my two teams coming out 1st class gunners; the last lot I put through were pretty successful. In about a week's time Bert and I have to go through a physical jerks and bayonet fighting course. The other two instructors are going through theirs now. I'll be pretty busy during the short time that is left before we go to the front

Yes, Dad, we are going very shortly – and about time, too! The Anzacs in the trenches want to know who is going to declare war first, Greece or our division. They also want to know where the lost division is; rubbing it in, aren't they? But even if we have been here quite a long time, we have been working hard and I hope that in the next 'Big Push' you will have news of good work done by the 43rd.

I, also, was wishing that I could be with you all on the 11th, but you know I was there in spirit, don't you, Dad?

We get papers here night and morning, so we are able to follow the progress of our side alright

I'm glad the prospects for the harvest at home are good, and trust that all hopes in that direction will be fulfilled. If conscription eventuates, I do hope the young married fellows won't be called in, for I reckon they are all wanted to carry on at home, don't you?

I think I have received all the letters that have been sent from home. Every mail I receive a big budget full of news and brimming over with love. I can tell you it bucks a fellow up and I'm sure it will help me when I am in the firing line. I know that you are all praying for my safety and I do want to get back home again. I want to prove myself a real fighting Anzac and to be ready and able to do my bit when the crucial hour comes. I am quite ready for whatever is in store for me, whatever the issue. So <u>don't</u> <u>worry</u>, any of you, but be of good cheer, whatever happens to me. You bet your life I'll always be in good spirits.

Au Revoir, Dad,
Yours Lovingly,
"Theo"

Lark Hill Camp
Salisbury Plain
<u>England</u>
23/10/16

Dearest Loved Ones,
I haven't any news to interest you this time; everything has been rubbing along in the same old way. Preparations for departure are, of course, under way and we are very busily occupied. This morning we commenced instructing another school, but owing to our early departure the time for the course has been curtailed.

On Thursday and Friday last we put the last school through their firing classification and in my squad of thirteen, only two failed to become 1st class gunners. For a wonder, it forgot to rain on both days, but it was bitterly cold out on the open plain.

On Saturday, the 11th Brigade was inspected by Staff Officers to find out its fitness, but the parade was nothing out of the ordinary so there's no need to go into details. Sunday I spent doing some washing, which took quite a long time, and having a lazy time inside. I'm in the habit of being in bed about 8 p.m. lately, just fancy that!

A mail closes at 2.30 p.m. today and I just heard of it as I am endeavouring to just scribble a few lines to tell you how I'm going. As usual I'm in the best of health and spirits, and looking forward to receiving the next Australian mail.

We boys were expecting to have our leave granted as from today, but find that we can't get away until next Friday. We had a kit inspection on Saturday and all clothing unserviceable is to be replaced, so we will be well fitted out when we leave here. We have had issued to us a bonnie heavy pair of boots, which are very solid and serviceable and good for marching in, altho' at the end of a march they feel about a tone weight until one gets used to them.

I must say *Au Revoir* and try and get a few lines written to Ivey. So goodbye for this time.
With fondest love and kisses to each one.
Yours Lovingly,
"Theo"

Wootten's Hotel
Waterloo Road
London
<u>England</u>
30/10/16

My dearest Loved Ones,
Contrary to expectations my holidays are once again being spent in this great city, the reason being that Mr. Tucker (Ivey's coz.) wrote to me on Thursday saying that measles had broken out in their school and they purposed going away for a short time, but would be more than glad to see me when they returned. Goodness knows where I shall be then! I was deeply disappointed at being done out of the happy time which I had pictured myself having; but perhaps another chance will occur later.

So instead, of going to Calne I came to London instead,

leaving Amesbury by troop train on Friday at 10.15 a.m. Got here after about 8 hours run and spent a long time looking around for lodgings without success; suddenly we thought of the ranch at which we stayed on our last visit, and were able to get a nice room for the two of us. In the evening we had a bit of fun at a fun parlour where we tried to beat each other at various games and feats of strength. From there we went to the pictures and were quite ready for bed when we got back to the hotel about midnight.

On Saturday we set out about 10.15 a.m. – late as usual – and walked to Trafalgar Square via the Strand, then up Tottenham Court Road to Hyde Park; we sat down for a time and watched the rich folks doing their morning constitutional per motor car, carriage and horses and on horseback. Having read of these things it was good to see them in real life. Beautiful women, luxurious motors, beautifully appointed carriages, liveried footmen, etc., and the finest of horses. We soon got tired of this and walked round Park Lane, had dinner at the Marble Arch Café; inspected the Marble Arch, and then boarded a bus, which took us out to the Flying School at Hendon. But that was nothing new for us for I have already told you of the great flying school on the plain.

We spent the evening mixing with the crowds in the main thoroughfares and inspecting shop windows; later on we found ourselves at the fun parlour in the Strand, so we spent quite a long time there having a good time. Sure we were quite ready for bed when we got back here. London is of course in comparative darkness at night. I hope I shall be able to see it when the streets are ablaze with light.

Yesterday we only visited two places – the Zoo and the Crystal Palace. We found our way to the Zoo after many enquiries and after hopping on and off quite a few buses. It was a long ride through unfamiliar streets. The Zoo gardens are beautifully laid out and are on a vast scale, altho' we wandered about for quite a long time, visiting the homes of various animals, etc. In the case of many of the animals, such as bears, mountain goats, sea lions, etc., efforts have been made to make their surroundings as near their natural environment as possible. A miniature mountain with terraces and tunnels for housing were provided for the bears and goats; the sea lions had their swimming pool and rocky homes. By Jove, these beasts can swim! The reptile house was very oppressive - like a hothouse, and there were all sorts and sizes of snakes from the giant Indian python to the very small species. The monkeys were good fun and, in one cage in particular, the inmates were very playful and had poles, a ball and swinging ladder to play on; they were doing all sorts of tricks. One little ginger-coloured fellow was especially funny.

As we were leaving the Zoo we met and chatted for a few minutes with an Australian nurse who had been in Egypt and was on furlough from France. Boarding a bus, which took us back to the centre of things once again, we got on to a Crystal Palace bus. After a long ride through some nice residential quarters we arrived at the palace only to find that the Navy men on guard there required a special permit for admission. This vast glass structure was a wonderful sight from outside and we were sorry that we could not see what it contained.

Back again here to Waterloo Road we had tea, then, having got in a supply of fruit, commenced letter writing. I believe this is the Xmas mail so I take the opportunity of wishing for you all the good things that you may want, and the greatest of all – health and happiness. I would dearly love to send along as Xmas gifts some of the beautiful things one sees, but finances won't permit. Once more, I wish you, every one, the season's greetings.

With fondest love to each and all of you,

Yours lovingly,

"Theo"

Lark Hill Camp
Salisbury Plain,
<u>England</u>
5/11/16
My dearest Loved Ones,

The Australian mail came to hand today, after being at headquarters for a week, the staff couldn't handle it until the outgoing mail to the 'Sunny South' was off their hands. So every day this week we have hoped the letters would be given forth, only to be disappointed. But everything comes to those who wait – if they wait long enough!

Mother darling, that was a beautiful long letter which you wrote me and it made me very happy – 'twas the one dated 19/9/16. Many of the queries, etc., will have found an answer in letters that you will have received long since. Mail days are the best days of all for us, you know. This time in addition to your loving one, and Daisy's, Millie's and Laurie's, I received others from Gawler, Phil, Frank and Harvey, but none at all from my sweetheart. I must not worry though, for I know that she would not miss writing in any case, and several of our letters have lately been going first to the 11th Machine Gun Company!

Our work is now ended. We put the last batch through their firing classification on Wednesday and Thursday last, and spent a couple of wet miserable days on the ranges. Out of twenty four men on my gun only three failed to become 1st class gunners and they only missed it by five points. On Friday we spent the day in the hut hearing lectures given by our beloved Sergt. Les. Rayner. Yesterday was spent in various duties and today it has been wet and stormy; we have been in the hut all day reading books and letters and writing, etc.

For the last week a Zonophone,[61] lent to us by the padre, has been going without a stop practically from Reveille to Lights Out. We have a heap of records of excellent hymns, instrumental pieces, some very good songs and comics; the sound of these has been wonderfully cheering. Many of the pieces take our thoughts back to home and loved ones and the hymns remind me of the singsongs we used to have.

I did not know till this afternoon that a mail goes tomorrow – I was caught napping. I was allowing for the 15th. Will write more fully then. *Au Revoir* dearest Mother, Father, sisters and brother, with greatest love and heaps of kisses,

From,

"Theo"

P.S. – I've sent envelopes containing P.C.'s to Mother, Father and Laurie. I'm sorry to say yours have been mislaid, Mill; look out for next mail.

Lark Hill Camp
England
6/11/16

Dear Mrs. Wright,

I was so pleased to receive a letter from you yesterday. It made me feel quite pleased with myself to think I had enlisted and so met you all. You were, and are still, all so kind to me, and I do so much appreciate all you have done for me. But I am always a poor one to make myself understood. Parting is very hard, and although I didn't say anything, I thought a lot. I am so thankful for that final handshake from you, and your few words conveyed such a lot; they are a big help to me. Theo is

---

61 Very similar to a gramophone for playing music recordings.

a good boy, and he thinks the world of his mother, and I am so pleased to have him for a pal.

I received a letter from my mother yesterday, the first for a long time. She is a dear little woman, but I think worries a lot. Theo hasn't been too well of late. He has a cold and sore throat. Yesterday he received some medicine from the doctor and he seems a lot better today. I think almost everybody in our section has had a cold of late. I am not rid of mine myself, yet.

I was so sorry to hear of the death of one so dear to you all.[62] It must be very sad. Only yesterday I had a letter saying an uncle had been killed, and a cousin wounded. We didn't seem to know how well we were off until this terrible war came about. But it's a great help to know we have the Lord as our saviour.

I haven't met Mr. Daenke yet, but will try and find him. As a rule soldiers don't need any introduction. We were expecting to move to France this week, but the time has been postponed again. Our chaplain told us, we will most likely be moving in another three weeks time.

It has been very wet here all last week and it is still raining. I have told Millie most of the news, so I won't repeat it again.

I am so pleased to have heard from you.

Trusting that you are all well.

I shall close,

With best wishes to all,

From,

Yours Sincerely,

Bert Westley

---

62 Bert Westley is referring to the death of Alice Wrights foster father – William Blunden.

<u>France</u>
Nov 12th '16
Dear Mr. & Mrs. Wright,

I am very pleased to be able to write to you again. There is very little of interest for one to write about from here, but I know you will pardon me on that score. Firstly, I must thank you for sending me the September *Chronicle*, which I have just received. The last four months I have been rather unfortunate in not receiving my mail, but I hope to be more fortunate from now on.

I have again rejoined my unit and have been with them about a week. We are resting in billets well in rear of the line and the boys can well do with it as they have been having a very rough time lately. The particular part of the Front they were last in is the worst on the line, and they came out in a fearful condition. It was rather difficult to know whether they were made of mud or ordinary human beings; a great deal of the time they were standing in water and mud past the knees and it was very wet and cold. As you can see the conditions were by no means the best. I am very thankful to say I missed that turn, but have a great chance of catching the same again in a few days time.

There is one good point about our boys and that is, you cannot break their spirit. We have some very rough times and do a certain amount of complaining while undergoing them, but give the boys a few hours rest and a few good meals and they are ready to undergo the trials again. We were hoping to be relieved from the trenches for the winter, but General Birdwood, this morning at Church Parade, gave us to understand that there was little hope of it coming about. Anyway whatever we may have to do we will get through alright I expect. We are all still hoping for the best.

I have quite recovered from my wound and am keeping in the best of health. I had a splendid time while in England and on my furlough in Scotland. The people are very homely and give we Australians a really good time. Great praise is due to people there for their untiring efforts. The Tommies, too, are fine fellows; since coming in contact with them we have completely changed our views of them and I am pleased to say that today there are very few Australians who are prejudiced against them as of old.

It gets dark very early here now so I must close. I hope before long we may all have a chance of meeting again. Although a little late I wish all the best greetings of the season.

I am,
Sincerely your friend,
Jack.[63]

Lark Hill Camp
Salisbury Plain
England
Nov.12th, 1916

My dearest Loved Ones,
Another 'Aus' mail came to hand yesterday and I received a nice little budget of eight; two from Ivey this time, presumably the one that should have come to hand last time; letters from Mother, Daisy, Mill and Laurie, Phil, Coz. Nel,[64] Tiny Seacombe and a bundle of *Stars* which I have not yet opened – quite a nice little mail to keep me pleasantly occupied for a time and to fill my mind with fresh thoughts of home and loved ones.

There's something I have not told you in the last couple of letters, which I suppose I may as well do so, but you must not worry about such things. When Bert and I returned from London about midnight a fortnight or so ago, we found that the

63 Jack Carr – a cousin to the Wrights.

64 Cousin Nel.

Lewis gunners had shifted their quarters. As it was too late to wander about the camp looking for them we lay down on the floor of an adjacent hut to our old one, which was occupied by scouts. I collared an extra overcoat, but owing to the cold and the fact that we had been pretty well soaked on our walk from Amesbury station, sleep was out of the question. The night seemed pretty long, but passed at last.

Next morning we found that our section had been isolated, as one of the boys had been removed to the hospital suffering from meningitis, though only slightly. The isolation was not very strict owing to the case not being a serious one, and we instructors were allowed to carry on with our work, for that could not be stopped as time was precious; but others had a holiday for a week. We had to have our throats swabbed and each day we had nasal douches and throat gargle. The padre lent us a Zonophone and 'tis a wonder the old thing survived for it was going practically all the time from Reveille to Lights Out and gave us a great amount of pleasure; the accompanying pile of records consisted of classical songs, comics, some of the most beautiful hymns and instrumental pieces, etc. You can understand that it would be going continuously under the circumstances and lots of the pieces took us back to the "Sunny South", where I enjoyed the memory of many happy singsongs.

Well, the wetting I received that Monday, and with Wednesday and Thursday spent on the ranges I gained a bonza dose of the flu, but 'tis gradually getting better. The boys have been laughing at me because my voice 'went on furlough' for a day or two. I have been in bed almost directly after tea every night this week, so have been looking after myself as much as possible. You bet I don't invite trouble, but in this life all things cannot be guarded against. You must not worry though, for there's nothing to worry about. Just about everyone in the battalion is similarly affected.

You know that I have said that I did not see Ally Daenke after landing in England; well, this morning when we marched on to the general parade ground there were fifty or sixty men standing by their kit bags there, proclaiming the fact that they were reinforcements. I saw Ally amongst them and happened to catch his eye. These chaps have been brought from another camp in order to make up the strength of the battalion. I have not dropped across him during the day, but I guess they have spent a busy day getting fixed up and assigned to the different companies – I hope that we shall see a good deal of each other in future.

Nothing very newsy has happened to us this week. With the exception of one day spent in field firing practice on the ranges, we have spent most of the time inside the hut owing to the inclemency of the weather, and there our favourite Sergt., Les Rayner, gave us a series of instructive lectures on various subjects. During the week we have also had new underclothing issued to us; so we are being fitted up well before we go to France. Very few articles are taken away with us: a few under garments, shaving kit, cap comforter, towel, soap, overcoat and waterproof sheet are about all the extras we take and they have all to go into our pack – some task to get 'em all in, I reckon! All other articles are packed in the big kit bag and left behind somewhere.

Mother dear, I did receive the beautiful letter of seven pages, which came by the last mail, and I have read it through not only once, but many times. I have just been through my pockets in the effort to find it in order that I might reply to various queries, but have discovered that 'tis not in any of my multitudinous pockets – I guess I have put it in some safe place. Therefore I must rely on my memory. It must have taken you a long time to write it, dear, judging by the time it takes me to get through my correspondence. *I remember you telling me before of that critical period of my babyhood and I'm afraid I have been disposed sometimes to wish that I had not lived. But not of late years!* You see I have got something to live for and fight for now, if I never had before; and I think of late years I have shown a tendency towards improvement – anyway, I have battled against various Old Nicks in my system and I'm a little bit better for it I hope. I don't think this chap is of the stamp to do anything more than his fellows, although I'd like to do something to make my loved ones proud to own me. Anyway, if I can play the game and get back home again I shall be satisfied.

To know that the souvenir of Egypt found such great favour in your eyes fills me with delight; I daresay it would not look so bad inside a frame, all serene, eh? That's good! I have been looking forward to receiving another such letter from you, dear old Dad, as the one, which you wrote me from Willunga. I do hope that the silver Machine Gun Corps badge does not prove a bit big for a tiepin, but the mere fact that you have been wearing it proves that it must be alright. I guess it will be a coincidence if you ever run across another person with a similar tiepin. (My fountain pen has been up to tricks and I have just taken it to pieces and cleaned it up a bit. Hope it goes A.1. now.) The pen has been of the very greatest value to me, Dad, and will be so right through the chapter; those ink pellets, Mill are bonza – abso(bally)lutely! I think I have made the ink a bit thick though this time, I'm afraid!

I can quite understand that Ted cannot join up, Mother, and now that conscription is off there will be no anxiety on that score. Speaking generally, if reinforcements don't come to hand I guess it will mean a harder time for the Australians who are in the trenches. There won't be men to take their places eventually when their turn for a spell comes and they will be compelled to put in a longer period. That, I do believe, will be the result of the win of the 'Noes'. Reinforcements that have lately come over from South Australia, are being eaten up by the battalions of the other States besides our own. I am afraid that the referendum caused a great deal of strife in our fair land; what a pity that such things should be when the struggle against our great enemy is at such a critical stage. The latest rumour we hear, is that there is a big coal strike in Australia – I do hope 'tis not true.

I do hope that Ted and Dais may be left together in happiness. At first I was going to vote 'No' because I was thinking of such as they; but on learning that young married men were not liable, and looking at the matter from various standpoints, such as the instance above, I plumped for Yes.

I am glad that Ivey's folks and mine are becoming so well acquainted. I hear that the little girls were enraptured with Laurie's doll. The public school children's concert must have been delightful. There's nothing like a kiddies' concert, after all, is there? Sure, Bert and I are as good pals as ever we were and the 'we', whenever stated, means 'Bert and Theo'. Now I hope that I shall be able to welcome Ally into the 'brotherhood', but that depends where he will be placed. He won't be able to get into our lot because all the training for gunners has been completed and we are full up.

That is a natty badge, dear ones, and it has been placed in my pocket book amongst my treasures, in fact the pocket book is becoming so bulgy that it takes a bit of scheming to get the catch to fasten.

It is just lovely for me to know that you all love Ivey so, I can tell you, and it's mighty good to think that she can be often with you.

I'm so sorry to hear about Aunt Jane.[65]

Not to be able to meet old Alan again here below doesn't seem as if it can be true. You remember what great pals we were and can imagine how greatly saddened I was to hear that

---

65 3 lines are blotted out here either by Theo or the censor.

he has gone to answer the 'Big Roll Call'. He was a dear old boy and well liked by his men, I believe, and I am sure his reward will be great.

Of course the home folks are 'worth while' – there is no place like home and no folks like the dear ones there. When writing home, and to Ivey, I always try and give you the best letters of which I am capable, because my small efforts are very poor in comparison with what is due to such loving ones. You are all very dear to me, as you know.

You all write such bonza letters, flowing over with love that I should love to write you each a separate one in return; perhaps some of you are disappointed when, after writing so many loving epistles you don't get one in return, or perhaps one of you may get one and not another. Also, I may sometimes fail to mention some of you when writing. Supposing that may be so, don't think hardly of me for it, but try and place yourself in my place, with a limited amount of time at my disposal and perhaps tired out after an arduous day's work and with a big mail to answer. You'll agree that it's a big proposition. It always takes a very long time to write my two love-letters – the home letter and Ivey's - and after that I have to do the best I can. When reading the home letter, each one of you, try and think that it is written just for you and in reply to yours.

You all write such bonza letters – Mother, Father, Bert and Ron, Fred and Evelyn, Con and George, Dais, Mill and Laurel - and I can assure you I read them all greedily and prize the contents. You see I'm not over here on a picnic; I'm on a big job and have plenty of work to do. It isn't as if I was on a holiday. Then I should feel it a matter of honour to reply to each one, but placed as I am I think you will allow that I've done pretty well as far as writing goes. Now, no reference has been made regarding the above but I thought that there may be a little hurt lying in some of your breasts, so I thought I'd just open up a bit on the subject. Do you get me?

After leaving here, opportunities for writing may be scarce, time will tell. But you bet I'll write as much and as often as possible.

The badge has imprinted on it the wrong colours – chocolate and light blue are the correct ones. They've just been issued. I'd like to send you a sample; don't know if it is possible, though.

Au Revoir, dearest Mother, Father, Bertha, Ron, Con, George, Evelyn, Fred, Dais, Ted, Mill and Laurie, and little nieces and nephews. You'll soon be hearing from me from France, I hope.

Very fondest love and heaps of kisses to each one of you, from,
Lovingly Yours,
"Theo"

Larkhill Camp,
Salisbury Plain
England
22/11/16
My dearest Loved Ones,

This time I am really and truly writing just prior to our departure from these shores, presumably bound for France. Of late our time has been spent making preparations for going away and you can bet we have been busily occupied. Also the route marches and various stunts have been both numerous and strenuous and they have been carried out to the satisfaction of the divisional heads.

The weather of late has been very miserable. Cold, rain and snow – a combination which I had not before experienced, and I can assure you I have not fallen in love with it. Take Friday last, for instance, as we marched away from camp it was bitterly cold and remained cold all day and at night just a few straggly flakes of snow fell. The intense cold continued on

Saturday and in the afternoon the flakes of snow began to grow larger and denser in volume until at night there was sufficient lying around to supply a few snowballs.

On Sunday morning when we poked our heads outside the door of the hut it was the signal for a bombardment by the early risers and soon snowballing scraps were going on all over the camp. Officers and anyone and everyone were 'topped off' as they passed to and fro. The officers, too, were having high jinks at their own quarters. The men behaved just like kiddies and entered into the sport just as one reads so often about it in books. Snowmen of all sorts, shapes and sizes dotted the vicinity of the camp and several giant balls of snow were moulded and rolled slowly along, growing larger as they progressed on their way. Sure, the fun was fast and furious while the snow lasted. But about dinnertime the air grew just a trifle warmer and the snow began to thaw and very soon, in place of the beautiful white soft mantle, which had previously clothed this old earth of ours, there were a few inches of slush where the passage of many feet worked it up. Winter, after giving us a fleeting glimpse of her face, fled back from whence she came, apparently ashamed of making her appearance too soon. The succeeding days have been growing gradually warmer, while today Old Sol[66] showed us his smiling face to give the assurance that he had not yet left us to the mercies of his rival – Winter!

On Saturday night a sergeant brought me a message from Capt. Stewart, who was at the officers' quarters, saying that he would see me at 9 a.m. Sunday. You bet I was up at his room punctually Sunday and had a short chat with him (or, rather, I tried to talk). Although my cold is slowly getting better, my voice seems reluctant to return to duty. As it has been absent without leave too long now, I shall have to deal severely with it on its return.

---

66 A reference to the sun especially in Roman mythology.

Today, as there has been instructing to do, one of the Sergeants took my place and I have done nothing all day – just been a looker-on, had a good spell and smoked when I could sneak the opportunity. Guess it will be a like program tomorrow. 'Tis just a final brush up for a few of them, only in loading and firing the gun.

Sunday night I wrapped myself up well and accompanied Bert and three other mates – Harry Cook, Percy Johncock (two Mt. Barker boys) and Harry Symonds (he is a Kent Townite) of our A.M.C. In chatting, Harry and I found that we knew several mutual friends. He is also intimate with the Billings at Malvern. Although I've known Harry some time, neither of us had any idea that the other knew Kent Town Church, and Kent Town folks.

The service at Durrington Congregational Church was conducted by a British Tommy who gave us a good address, but I can't remember the text, for it was rather a long one. At the conclusion of the usual service, a prayer and praise meeting was held, so as it was our last opportunity of so doing we stayed until the finish, and were glad that we did so. A number of the boys who were leaving during the week were present at the service and my only regret was that I could not join in the singing. The many helpful texts, quotations and loving advice, which your letters have contained, dearest Mother, I have tried to follow out, and will continue to try to do so.

It has been lovely beyond words to receive the many budgets of letters overflowing with love and interesting news from each one of you from home. I trust that no hitch will occur in their dispatch henceforth. But that is not likely. The only mails that have failed to reach us are those, which went down with the *Arabia* – and that's one that we have to get even with the 'squareheads'[67] for. If the *Arabia* had passed untouched we

---

67 Referring to the German race.

would have had messages from home coming to us just prior to our departure; now we will be in France for a while before we get any news.

As we have not been paid right up-to-date, as we expected would be the case, one or two little things which I wanted to purchase and send along home, will have to be held over until Providence extends to me another opportunity of returning here. What with buying up medicine, etc., I couldn't manage it. I haven't got much faith in the medicine we get from the doctor. I would prefer some of the old-time remedies. Don't think I'm ill, 'cos I'm not; the cold is only the ordinary common garden variety and will work off as the others have done.

I didn't think I had much news when I started, but I have worked from one subject to another until a letter of sorts has resulted.

Now, my dearest Mother, Father, Bert, Ron, Con, George, Fred, Evelyn, Dais, Ted, Mill, Laurie, nieces and nephews, I must bid you a fond *Au Revoir*. Don't worry about me; the machine gun officers are 'topnotchers' and are well loved by us. They will look after our welfare as far as lays in their power. In the event of you hearing any bad news about me, don't give credence to it until you get news from the right quarter. I'm going into this final flutter with a light heart and the hope that I will make good; back of all is the vision of a glorious return to home and loved ones.

With best love and kisses,

Yours. Lovingly,

THEO

P.S. While my assistant is carrying on with the instructing I must take the opportunity of telling you something which I know you will be extremely glad to hear.

You know that I have been hoping for some time past that I should get another stripe, well, my luck has at last taken a turn for the better; now I am Corporal Theo, eh what! Just a short while ago word was sent to where we are instructing that we three Lance Corps. were wanted by the O.C. On reporting to him, we were paraded before the Colonel, who informed us that as Mr. Osborne had recommended us, we were raised to the rank of corporal, each to be in charge of a gun and team. Then followed some instructions and advice and then – About turn! Quick march! Out of his august presence!

Our responsibility will now be pretty great and I will often be left to my own resources – I'm going to make good. I'll now have to study tactics pretty hard in the short time before we get into the dinkum thing. But now a chap has some encouragement to make every endeavour.

The Colonel said great things are expected of the Lewis Gunners! Now my pay will be greatly increased, and that is an exceedingly gratifying aspect of the case. The promotion dates from today.

Once again, *Au Revoir* and the very best of fond love from "Theo"

Somewhere in France
December 7th, 1916
Dear Lez, Nell and Frank,[68]

I was greatly pleased to receive your letters just before leaving England and to know that things are going pretty well up there. At the time of writing Australia was in the throes of the conscription campaign, but now that has been turned down. You spoke as if you intended joining up but being an old married man you ought to stay at home, Frank. As you may guess I have written a number of letters while in England and

---

68 Cousins

as I never keep a tally of those to whom I write I can't think when I last wrote to you.

I cannot give any details of my doings for we have had orders issued that letters must be short. Life in England was lovely in the summer and during our four days leave in London at the beginning of August we were favoured with beautiful weather and had a bonnie time – the people (especially the girls) like Australians. Later on I spent a weekend there and a short time before coming over this side we were granted another four days leave. So after three visits I began to know the napes a bit. I saw most of the historical places including the Tower of London (on our last trip) where our eyes were dazzled by the splendour of the Crown Jewels. That's only one of the many sights.

I am just imagining myself back at the 'Burg at this time of the year and trotting off down to pay a weekend visit to you; or else down for an afternoon of tennis with Trix and Dolly. They were good times! Since your news of Hurtle, I heard that he had been killed; his cousin, after making enquiries received that information. Hurtle had a good innings, didn't he – right through Gallipoli and a long time in France. Word has just been received that the letters we are writing are too long, so I must sign off for this time and tell you more later on. The mails received and forwarded to Australia are stupendous – you bet we are happiest when we get letters from the Sunny South. By the way ask Miss Hilda if a German 'souvenier' will do instead of a 'Turkish fez'. You see, I haven't forgotten –
Love from Theo.

PS
Give the little girls, Jean and Madge, a kiss from me and tell them I want another little letter soon.

Somewhere in France
Dec. 8th, 1916

My dear Mill & Laurie,
You both wrote such bonza letters this mail that I must drop you a few lines and as our correspondence is curtailed you must share this epistle.

While I think of it, Harold Daenke[69] is in 'A. Coy'[70] of our battalion; as we are attached to the same company, we are now able to see a great deal of each other. He told me today that he had received a letter from Ted, but it had been written in September and had been chasing him around.

It is very good of you both to write fully of all the home news and if I can't reply to all queries, etc., don't think that I don't notice them. It's because I can't do so.

Bert received your diary today, Mill; 'tis O.K. I was told there was nothing for me but have learnt since that mine is at the headquarters and you bet I shall be off up there for it tomorrow.[71]

That was a jolly good description of the schools concert, Laurie dear. In fact, 'tis hard to believe that those letters you write come from the 'young un' – my baby sister!

We go into an adjacent village pretty often and have a feed of fried eggs and chips – not because we are ill fed, but just as a top-off, like. We have no cause for complaint re food.

It was very good of Mrs. G. to be enquiring about my welfare. 'Tis nice to know that all my friends seem to be remembering me. I had a very nice letter from Dorrie last mail, too. In it she said Dave was missing. Evidently they had not heard of his death. It was good to hear that Hurtle was not killed. I had

---

69 Harold Daenke, Brother of Fred Daenke who married Margaret (Millie Wright)

70 A company.

71 Theo wrote frankly in this diary and the entries are included later in this text.

word from his cousin that he had gone under and am mighty glad that 'tis not true.

I guess you all looked very sweet on the 11th; as most of you told me details of it, I received an excellent report of the wedding.

I'm glad that you folks and Hastwell's seem to be good friends – as you know they are sterling friends of mine. Glad to hear of Horace's success. You bet I appreciate the great kindness of you all with regard to Birthday cake and parcels, etc. Please convey to Bert and Ron my very best thanks re cake and to all the others, also. Ron was a brick to take the job on when he was so unwell. I'm glad the lawns and garden at home have come on so well – guess I won't know the old home when I get back.

Dais is lucky if she has the best boy that ever was, eh Laurie. Yes, thanks, the *Chronicles* come along alright and are A.1. You will have read about our experience of snow, 'young un'. What have you been doing to poor Smut? I'm glad you are looking after Ivey well, and 'tis good to know that she is bonnie and well. Sorry, I didn't know about Bob Boyce. We were near Bulford camp. I hope your cold is quite alright ere this, Laurie dear. Don't forget I am expecting to see my baby sister a big strong girl when I get home again.

I've written more than I intended and must stop now and say *Au Revoir*. With heaps of love to all of you at home and those at Prospect, Gawler, Strath and Pinnaroo. Ta! Ta!
Your Loving Bro.
"Theo"

p.s. I'll try and write a few lines to all the others next time.

"Somewhere in France"

My dearest Homefolks,
Here we are at last in the vicinity of one of the battlefronts. As I write I can hear the rumble as each side flings compliments to the other. We don't expect to go up to the trenches for some little time, yet.

A couple of days after our arrival a tremendous amount of mail and parcels arrived. I received about 13 or more letters – three lovely ones from you, Mother-mine, dated the 3rd, 6th and 20th of Oct., three from Mill (16th and 20th and 3rd Oct.), three from Laurie (3rd, 17th and 21st Oct.), Daisy (4th), Con and Mavis (15th), Fred (16th), Bert (16th), others from Phil and Mrs. H., Auntie Liz and Frank, Belle, Mill Clark and Dorrie Badger, and of course one from my sweetheart. All the letters were bonnie and it's simply grand to receive them – too lovely for words. I should like to reply to each one, as nicely as you wrote me but orders have been issued that all letters must be very short and also the hours of daylight at our disposal are very limited.

The many reports of the wedding, which I received, enabled me to see it almost as vividly as if I had been present. I'm sure you all looked very charming. I do not need to see any of you under extra special conditions to be proud of any of you. Your letters, dearest Mother, were very loving and beautiful and exceedingly helpful. I'm glad you got the extra size enlargement. I wish I could speak to you actually, Mother dear, and comfort you when you feel troubled about me. I am A.1. in health, good spirits and enjoying the life. We are a happy family in our barn home even though it is rather well ventilated for this climate.

Regarding clothes, we were well fitted out before leaving England and things are so organised that we get a hot bath and a change of clothes at regular intervals. Socks though are always welcome. I hope, Laurie dear, that I will be able to wear your first pair. Mill, does Ivey work at Sands & Mac's? In looking over one of your letters just now, something you said made me think so. You know an Australian mail went down with the *Arabia* and all I know is that Ivey now goes to business – somewhere.

Say, Dad, hurry up and write me another nice long letter. I want to hear all about Willunga. I'm very glad indeed to know that you like it so much there and that the change has done you such a lot of good.

In every mail I have received a budget of letters from you all, and so far as I know none have gone astray; I don't expect any difficulty in getting them even now. Parcels have not yet been delivered – there's such a pile of them!

From the bottom of my heart I thank you all so much for your efforts re parcels and I hope they'll come along soon.

I must close now, so *Au Revoir* and heaps of fondest love to each one. Be of good cheer, Mother-mine! No need to worry,
Yours Lovingly,
"Theo"

Somewhere in France
16-12-16

A surprise has been sprung on us – a mail closes for Australia tonight and I have only a very, very short time to get my letter written.

Nothing very startling has occurred since I last wrote a week or so ago. A couple of fine days occurred during the week, and when Old Sol shows his face there is always a very obvious activity of aircraft and the shelling of same by antiaircraft guns, etc. Two or three times this week we have seen aircraft manoeuvring over the lines; to us they appear only mere specks. For a time they will be seen travelling along at high speed and then small clouds of smoke will appear sometimes in a line and at others seeming to encircle the aeroplane. Of course we watch such events with interest but do not know if the planes concerned belong to our side or the enemy's.

We are becoming quite used to the sound of heavy gunfire and the rattle of machine guns, more especially at night. But we are some little distance behind the scene of operations. Soon, very soon I guess, we will be in amongst it, and we shall be glad too, to be doing something. One gets a bit stale when always at the same old routine.

During the last couple of days we have received mail from Australia and it brought me quite a pile of papers and a nice budget of letters. About Wednesday, I think it was, I received a parcel from home – it was a large round tin enwrapped with calico and containing many dainties for which I sincerely thank you all. The various tinned goods will be A.1. in the trenches and it was bonza to get the tobacco. After using issue tobacco I had quite a luxurious smoke. The cough jubes were just what I have been longing for. Now that I am O.K. again, I want to keep all coughs at a respectable distance. That's a pretty hard job though when one is drilling all day in mud and water and can't keep his boots dry. But a bit of a grumble is a soldier's privilege! No matter how nice things have been I notice there's always something to growl at!

All the home news is greedily devoured. I read with pleasure of your visit to Hastwell's. You should hear all the nice things they told me concerning my Mother and sisters! I'm so very, very glad to hear that Dad is still going strong – that health and business are both good. Dad, it was good-oh to hear from you again. The conscription referendum was a bad move, wasn't it? The cause of so much bitterness, etc.,

Mother-mine, your loving epistle was much enjoyed and also Mills', Laurie's and Bert's. As I have explained before, you must not be disappointed if you don't each receive an individual reply – it really can't be done. The same applies to queries, etc., but be sure I'm doing the best I can.

My health and spirits continue top-hole and your letters, bonnie Xmas greetings, parcels, etc., increase my happiness.

Must close now – with very fondest love and heaps of kisses to each one.

Your loving son and brother,

"Theo"

Somewhere in France
20-12-16
My dearest Homefolks,

Here I am still in the old barn where we have an abundance of fresh air! The weather does not get any warmer and yesterday the snow fell heavily and was followed by a sharp frost. Today the sun shone more brightly than he has done since our coming; as a result the fields made a pretty picture in the early morning before the snow commenced to thaw.

I've been having some shots with real bombs and rifle grenades during the last couple of days and I like it rather. Today the aircraft have been again very active, and the sight of an aeroplane encircled by a shower of bursting shells has been a common sight. The planes always seem to escape scatheless.

Tonight I made into a parcel the souvenirs for Mill and Laurie. I was unable to send them with the last letter. I hope the contents of the small package will meet with your approval, Mill and Laurie.

By the way, dearest Mother, you may be wondering since my promotion, the amount of my allotment money drawn by you should not be greater. But until I can get fresh allotment papers the money will remain owing to me. It won't make any difference; the amount I am entitled to and the sum drawn by me is shown on my pay-book and the pay-corporal knows all about it. I'm only going to continue on '2 bob' a day. Sure, I'll want all the 'bawbees'[72] I can muster when I get back home, eh! Thought perhaps I'd better mention this while I thought of it!

My health is <u>excellent</u>! Ditto, our food! But it's mighty cold; still we manage to keep warm and are becoming used to it by degrees.

Please tell Mrs. Hastwell, friends and others that we can only write a couple of letters per mail – maybe only one letter and one card soon – and as the loved ones at home and my fiancée always must come first, the others will have to get any news of me from you.

That's all for this time. Trust you are all well and happy. I am, (bet your life!). I shall think of you all gathered round the festive board on Monday next. I guess we will manage to have a merry time also, for we are a gay mob.
Fondest love to all and heaps of kisses,
Fondest Love –
"Theo"

Xmas Eve
<u>1916</u>
Dear Ones at Home,
Again we have only a few minutes to get a couple of lines written; we never seem to get decent notice of an outgoing mail now. Our thoughts are all with those at home today. Tomorrow we will have plum puddings, etc., so we will have a Xmas festival too. We are right up against one of the firing lines now; most of our chaps have been in the trenches doing fatigue work today – I wasn't wanted. Tell Ivey all the news please. I haven't time to write a letter to her now.
Fondest Love,
"Theo"

---

72 Treats, rewards.

Portrait of the Wright family taken circa 1912.
Left to Right: Bertha, Theo, Laurel (in front), Alice Jane,
Constance, Frederick, Joseph, Daisy and Margaret.

Theodore Willard Wright – 1911.

Dear All,

I was very pleased to receive the letters on Saturday
morning. So you have concluded the sale of the business' Well
I hope you are all satisfied now, and that your future efforts
with whatever end you may have in view, may be crowned with success. With regard to Daisy and Min, ie seeking situations in

town it would. I think, be nice for them if they could do so.
I can sympathise with them in not wanting to return to the Mt.,
for reasons which I think I have previously told you; then if
they were successful in obtaining good situations and ale-
able board and lodging, they would have a better cha-
afforded at Mount Gambier . What do
turn there, Dad? Will it not seem fu
town but not to the old home? It was
that the purchaser should be a broth-
it? I sincerely hope that the winding
satisfactoy to you. Do you mind tellin
on the stock; you see I was one of the
ago, so you mustn't mind, please, if I
about things, but you know I take a keen
on at home. I am very glad indeed that y
price for the pony, cart, etc.; polly mus
You don't seem to be giving yourselves an
arrangements as to what you will do when yo
home, or have you talked the matter over
actly what you are going to do I hope fo
the latter is the case. However, in whatev
you have my sympathy and best wishes for
wish it was possible for me to pay you a v
Oakbank, but I am afraid it is rather on
sible. At present I am the only one who
until Saturday last there was another you
good at the machine, although of course
and since my advent here he has helped m
wanted to get away any time, and he also
very often when I have been at work meals.
been of great help to me; so you see I
mained here perhaps it would have been possi
a trip to see you before you left, but I am afra
impossible.

I was busy typing this letter at 6 p.m. when Mr. Leicester ca
ed; he and Mr. Hass were waiting to take me for a drive out to
get a swarm of bees which we discovered yesterday some miles out
from here. We had not gone miles when a bonza thunder storm
storm came up, the lightning was very vivid, all descriptions of
aerial fireworks being displayed, but as we had a hooded trap it
was not quite so bad. However, it did not rain much as it happen
ed, and we secured the swarm without any mishap, by cutting off
the branch on which they were working and placing the part to
which the honeycombs was fixed into a box and shutting in the
bees by placing a bag over it. We had a nice drive home, the
rain making things very pleasant and cool. we did not arrive at
Petersburg till 9 o'clock and our landlady went up the pole
because we were so late in getting home to tea. As she has been
finding fault a good deal lately we are getting pretty tired of
being with Sinclair's, so don't be surpri _if I move off some
where else in the near future.

I might say that I have just called in (at 11 o'clock) to finish this that I can get it away to-morrow. As it is my first

Theo's type written letter to his family
(fragment).

Theo working at the printing press.

Theo with his fellow soldiers from the 43rd Battalion. (far left, middle row)

Theo Wright (front centre) taken shortly after enlistment in 1916. The scene is the Mitcham Army Camp located where the Adelaide suburb of Colonel Light Gardens is now situated.

Theo and his fellow soldiers in barracks at Salisbury Plain, enjoying their big budgets from home. (Theo far right smoking a pipe)

Somewhere in Belgium
July 29th, 1917.

My dearest Mother, Father Sisters & Brother:

It is probable that we shall be engaged in some pretty stiff fighting very shortly & as Bert W will not be going into the line this time, I am taking the opportunity of writing a note to you all which will be forwarded on to you, if it should happen that I am numbered amongst those who go under. Of course I am not expecting any such thing to happen, but I like to leave a note behind.

I have never regretted joining up, & I can truthfully say that I have enjoyed the life of a soldier. I have tried to play the game of life straight & clean & believe that I have succeeded.

The loving letters which I have received from you all have been very comforting. Believe me, your letters have been the best thing of all, & we always look forward longingly for Australian mail & are never so happy as when we get letters from the dear homefolk.

Don't mourn for me. I shall be happy to give my life for the cause, should the necessity arise.

In writing home I have tried to give you an idea of my doings since I left Australia & I trust that those letters have been a small source of

comfort to you, & help you to follow me in my journeyings to a certain extent, altho' the names of localities, etc. had of course to be omitted.

If Fate decrees that we are never again to meet in this life, there is comfort in the promise of a reunion in a far better land.

So, with my dearest love to you all — Mother Father Bert & Ron, Con & George, Fred & Evelyn, Dais & Ted Millie, Laurie, nieces & nephews, I say "Good-bye"

Lovingly Yours.
Theo

'Lovingly Yours' - Theo's last letter

Sergt E. A. WILLIAMS — Pte W. B. Thompson (from Truly)
(Queensland) (New Zealand)

"Somewhere in France"... June 17/1917

Theo (right) somewhere in France, with Sergeant E. A. Williams
and Private W. B. Thompson.

CORP THEODORE WILLARD WRIGHT
("THEO.")

Theo's Memorial Card

Memorial Display at the Mt Gambier Methodist Young Men's
Class. (Theo bottom, far left)

1917

COMMONWEALTH OF AUSTRALIA
SOUTH AUSTRALIAN RECRUITING COMMITTEE

Victoria Square
Adelaide
January 1917

Fellow Citizen,

Our State is in grave need of your services in the defence of her honour. She must provide at least sufficient volunteers to reinforce and relieve her own contingents at the front.

This can be done easily if eligible men like yourself will earnestly consider the actual danger that threatens our freedom in the possibility of a false peace, which could only be temporary and would allow Germany breathing time for more extensive preparations.

All the great authorities agree that deeper disaster would follow any truce between us and our foes. There is no middle course – we must destroy Prussian Militarism or IT WILL DESTROY US, and strangle the liberties of mankind.

The whole world is depending upon the shield of our Empire. With men and money forthcoming our victory is certain; if British men grow slack our doom is sealed. A recent cable states that a noted German who knows Australia has informed his countrymen that people in the Colonies degenerate and require new blood to maintain their form. Our men at the Front have nailed this lie. Will you join them in proving that the men still here have equal grit with those who have already shown their quality?

I appeal to your highest instinct. Lend your young energy to the noblest cause that ever called for men.

This letter will be followed by a visit from one of our Organisers, who will be proud and glad to welcome you as another volunteer.

I am, Fellow Citizen,

Yours faithfully,

(Sgd.) J. Newland,

Chairman

State Recruiting Committee.

Apply to:

F. A. Howland, (Col.)

Recruiting Officer

Australian Portable Diary 1917[73].
Theo. W. Wright.
No 937
Lance Corporal Theo. W. Wright
Machine gun Section
3rd Battalion
11th Brigade
3rd Division
        A. I. F.
    On Active Service
    October 11th 1916
From Millie, with heaps of Love and Kisses.

Notes from 1916

Movements of interest to be remembered:
Left Lark Hill, November 25th – passage across channel
The march to next camp at H-; couple of days train ride to B-,
then march to billets. March to firing line base (23). Experience
re working parties. Going into trenches on the morning of my
24th birthday. First nights experience. M.G.s[74]. Snipers, barbed
wire etc.

In the Trenches
Jan. 4th. 1917

My dearest Homefolk,
Before I go any further I must thank you from the bottom of
my heart for the bonza thought and the love that prompted you
to send the cable conveying greetings to me; you can't imagine
how delighted I was. So far as I know I enjoyed the distinction
of being the only gunner who received greetings by cable. I
was in such a hurry to scribble a few lines in order to send

73 Theo received a diary from his sister Millicent; his entries to this diary are included in *Italics*.

74 Machine Guns

away my last letter that when adding the short postscript I quite forgot at the time to thank you. There are so many things I wanted to say and so little time to say any of them that I quite omitted mention of it.

However, 'tis not too late now, and once more I tender to you my great appreciation of loving greetings. The cable was in plenty of time reaching me just before we left our first billets for others near the firing line.

The day prior to evacuating those billets Sir Douglas Haig[75] himself inspected us in review order. That day the weather turned out pretty nearly as beastly as possible over here and that is saying a great deal – plenty of water and mud to plough through and cold air that was anything but bracing. However, Sir Dug expressed himself as well pleased with our appearance. So that was alright!

The following day we packed our kit and set out on a few miles march to the billets that lie in the large town to the rear of our present position. The rain poured down nearly all the way and before we reached our destination the wind had reached the force of a hurricane, but we got there alright. We found the billets we were to occupy quite palatial in comparison to those we had left behind.

From this place we set out sometimes during the day and others at night, to do repair work in the trenches and clean silt from channels, which drain the water from the trenches. The latter work occupied us on Xmas Day. I wonder how you would like to have seen me in waders that reached to my thigh, over knee-deep in water shovelling silt from the channels. We N.C.O.s are sent up in charge of small parties of men and so do not have to work. However, 'tis better to work with the others and keep warm than to stand about in the cold. Working in the trenches at night isn't much of a game.

75 Sir Douglass Haig (1861-1928) – the most controversial of the war generals see http://www.firstworldwar. com/bio/haig.htm

I spent Xmas Day with a party cleaning out one of the channels and for our mid-day meal we lunched on bully beef and biscuits! Doesn't sound very festive, does it? Never mind, we quite made up for it when 'the toil of the long day was o'er' and we had wended our weary way 'homewards' – (What mockery!). Gee! But we did have a glorious tuck in! The cooks served up one of their most excellent stews – (and long practice has made them quite expert in that gentle art) which were followed by an appetising tinned Xmas pudding, nice and hot. It was a top-notcher, but not as good as the bonza ones that you know how to make, Mother-mine!

After a spell, which by the way was very necessary, I tackled some dessert in the way of biscuits, dates and lollies, followed by cigarettes and tobacco. For those who cared for it a pint of good beer was handed out. We had been promised a decent Xmas dinner and that which did come to light was lots better than even the best that I had expected. Don't you think we dined sumptuously? Of course our thoughts on that day were more than ever of home and loved ones and the many happy times spent about the festive board and the fond hope that next Xmas and for many succeeding years we would be spared to be with our dear ones. When our feast was at its height some of the officers came round and the toasts of 'The King', 'The Loved Ones at Home' and – 'Damnation to the Kaiser' we enthusiastically honoured. So you see, although we had a pretty hard day of it, the good things we found awaiting us more than made up for lots of things.

Jan. 6th 1917

Once more we are spending the night in billets after doing our short spell in the trenches. At last we have been under fire and no casualties occurred among the machine gunners; the battalion had only one killed and about half a dozen wounded. We went into the trenches in the dark hours of my birthday and it was jolly hard one getting there, too, loaded up with all our war material. Both sides did plenty of 'strafing'[76] and we got quite expert in dodging their various kinds of high explosives. I don't want to try and describe what it is like to you – I'll leave that till I come back! You will have read the experiences of any amount of others. We stood it A.1. and gave Fritz many thousands of rounds of ammunition – for we have a lot to pay him for!

In speaking to us today our O.C.[77] spoke highly of the way we did our job and said that everyone to whom he spoke has nothing but praise for us Lewis Gunners. Coming from the O.C. it was specially appreciated for he is not given to any soft-soaping.

Yesterday when we arrived in from the firing line, there were several parcels and papers for me. Parcels from Jean Bach, to which Mrs. Day and Mr. and Mrs. Bennett contributed; mittens from Gladys Ward; goods and hankies from Ivey; that bonza pair of socks from Laurie and also a pair from Bert's sister Lily. Just a bit of alright, eh! Your knitting, Laurie dear, is quite in keeping with your letters, excellent! I was just wishing for more socks and my wish was granted. Your letters, dearest ones, were just lovely, and I read them o'er and o'er. As letters have to be given in tomorrow night I'm afraid I won't be able to answer queries – may be able to do that in my next.

The registered parcels have not been given out yet. Don't be afraid of me not receiving letters and parcels – they all come in good time. Our boys here have received parcels galore altho' they are sometimes delayed. Please accept my loving thanks for all your many kindnesses and great love.

The Sergt. Major has just been in and I have to take a working party up to the firing line tomorrow – up at 3 a.m. and away at

76 Attack with machine guns or cannon fire from a low-flying plane

77 Officer Commanding

3.45. Won't have much time for writing tomorrow for we go for a bath and change of underclothes in the afternoon. I'm sitting up in bed writing this. 'Tis 8 p.m. so I must close and get a bit of sleep. *Au Revoir*, dear ones. Please tell my friends any news; I won't be able to write many letters nowadays. So ta! ta! all.

With very fondest love and kisses to each and every one from,
Your Loving Son and Brother.
"Theo"

Sunday. – Back alright from Front Line. Have just heard that there are more parcels at headquarters, guess mine from you are included.
Love, Theo.

In the Trenches
Somewhere in France
Jan. 16th, 1917

My Dearest Loved Ones,
Another Áussie mail is coming in driblets; I have received letters from Mother and Laurie, Dais and Ted, Phil Hastwell and am anxiously awaiting those from Ivey and Mill and all the others who usually write to me; guess they will come in good time.

Sure I'm stumped for news this time. Of course we are not allowed to say too much about what goes on in this quarter and there's very little else that one can put in a letter – so don't be disappointed if this epistle is neither very long nor very newsy.

We boys often wish we had some of the nice hot summer days of Australia over this way for it is so beastly cold – rain, sleet, snow and frost are frequent visitors of ours nowadays. We are warmly clothed, though, and make our quarters in the trenches as snug as possible.

The officers of the watch and N.C.O.s all make themselves at home in our joint. For the first few days we fared extremely well for we had a coke fire going and had porridge of a morning and, for dinner on three occasions, dined sumptuously on tinned plum pudding and blanc-mange, the latter being made by the cook of our outfit,

Always we bring in a pretty good stock of eatables for we are terribly big eaters and although the military give us a fairly good supply of tucker, they can't supply us with enough rations for us to be eating all day. With us 'tis just about a case of one meal a day – and that lasts all day. So that will show you that we are all very well and are doing well under these exceptional conditions. But, Jove! it is cold.

Thank you muchly, Mother-mine, for the news you give me about Ivey and 'tis bonnie to know that you all love her so! From Nov. 23rd you should receive allotments amounting to 6/6 per day. I did not get them to increase my daily allowance, for I shall want all the money I can raise when I return, I guess! I want to realise my ambition of getting on the linotype and may have to pay a premium in order to learn it. You see, although I am so many thousands of miles away trying to do my bit, I am planning in my mind what I intend doing when I get back

I must get a good substantial job if possible before I can ask Ivey to share my lot, eh?

I can picture you waiting for letters, mother dear; 'tis nice to know that my efforts to describe my doings and places visited please you so.

While we are in the Front Line, Bert and I are widely separated, being on opposite flanks of our particular frontage, so there's practically no chance of knowing how each is getting on until we move back from the Front Line, which we do at intervals. Yesterday, however, for the first time, Bert came around this way and we swapped the letters that we had received.

The other night we had our biggest "strafe". Talk about fireworks – it was some display I can tell you, but as I said before we have become rather expert in getting out of the way of Fritz's missiles. On this particular night we had only 5 men slightly wounded. Our battalion has been exceptionally lucky, for so far only one has been killed. Fritz has not caused our little section any loss so far and we are hoping that our luck will continue for some time to come.

I always look forward to mail days, you bet, and you are a dear, Mother, to always write such bonza long letters, I read them o'er not only once, but many times.

So sorry, dears, that sometimes there is a long period between the receipt of letters from me; but you know I always write. However, 'tis not surprising that some letters get delayed in transit for the mails to and from the soldiers is simply immense.

Now that we are opposite Fritz, letters may not reach you regularly at all, but I shall write at every opportunity, you know that, don't you? If there are times when letters are delayed longer than usual you must not worry – I've got a feeling that I shall come through this mix-up alright!

As usual I believe there are all sorts of rumours circulating in Australia with regard to our battalion – don't take any notice of rumours, treat anything that is not officially given out as mere piffle. Above all, don't worry about me. I am enjoying the life as much as 'tis possible so to do – but all the same, we are looking forward to the time when peace will be declared and we are allowed to return to home and loved ones.

Say, Dad! I hope you will be able to write me another letter soon. I wish you could write every mail, but I know what a hard worker you are, and can picture you poring over plans and making up estimates after a hard day's graft.

Sure, Laurie, the places I have seen somehow always appear different in reality to what I have imagined them to be. You bet, Australia is first every time – no country I have seen can come within "coo-ee" of the Land of the Southern Cross.

So, you are going in for pen painting 'Young Un'[78]. Good luck to you. That will be nice! That bazaar was a success right enough, wish I could have made some purchases at your stall.

Those socks arrived O.K. and have helped to keep my feet warm these freezing days and nights. I won't be surprised if I find the man on guard frozen at his post one of these nights, the cold is so intense.

Will say ta! ta! for the time being. Expect there will be more letters to answer yet.

20-1-17

Another batch of letters have arrived, bringing those tricks of doggie cards of Mills', bonza letter from Mother, Dad, Millie and Laurie and the photo of Betty and Rex.

My dearest thanks to all of you for your loving news. Bert,[79] dear, I do receive a letter from you every mail and trust I have not omitted to tell you before how I love to hear about what goes on in your particular sphere. The kids are wags and things they say make me laugh. Keep on doing it, Bert, old girl; your letters are just the thing.

I was so pleased, dear Dad, to hear from you that all is well with you and that you had finished up at Willunga. How lovely it must be for you all that you are home once again. I do hope that your health and your business will continue to go strong. Dad, I don't understand your reference to Sir Richard B. I know why I came over to 'try to do my bit' and even if there are those

---

78 Theo's pet name for Laurie/Laurel

79 Adeline Bertha, Theo's sister, married to Ron Osman

who don't want to come along, we are going to stick to the job. I love my work and – I'm here till my 'bit' is completed.

Don't be too severe on the boys, Dad. Many have done their bit and returned to civil life and cannot be picked out from the shirkers; also, one never knows what it is that prevents any other fellow from enlisting – he may be breaking his heart to get away and cannot. Fancy his feelings if he was accused of cowardice! You know I have been in a somewhat similar position myself and – I know!

Mother, Mill and Laurie, you have supplied me with heaps of news of your doings and it makes bonnie reading. I'm afraid if I made as much reference to various parts of your letters as I wished, the letter would not get through – it would be too bulky!

Bert and Ron, that photo of Rex and Betty[80] is A.1. Aren't they bonnie kids? Tell them I carry their photos in my breast pocket and am very proud of them, will you please?

Dais and Ted, I was delighted to hear from you and to know that you are so happy. Write often and tell me all about what goes on in your 'appy 'ome. Sure, I'm looking forward to the promised visit by Ivey and M.

Your letter, Dad dear, was dated 19-11-16, and Mother's dated 23-11-16. (Sorry but can't find the other letters; however, the dates were somewhere about then!) Oh, I just remember, Bert W. has those letters.

Today, Corp. Archie Fletcher, two gunners and I were detailed from the section to train for a special job; that means that we are in billets away from our own chaps. It won't be for long though – the work isn't very important, but it means a short spell from work in the trenches, and that is acceptable.

Say, Dad, the ground wears a mantle of snow nowadays and the cold is pretty severe for us. We are well looked after tho' and can stand it. Yes, Dad, I can imagine better now what your

80 The Osman children

life in America was. Sorry I haven't those other letters to refer to.

I'm in excellent spirits and as fit as a fiddle. <u>Don't</u> <u>worry</u> – this life rather suits me, and I'm just A.1. Nevertheless, my thoughts are always with you and I trust it won't be long before I'm back with you again.

I really must stop so ta! ta!

Lovingly yours,

"Theo"

<u>Somewhere in France</u>

Feb. 1st, 1917

My dearest Homefolk,

My last batch of mail brought along letters from Mother, Father, Bertha, Fred, Millie and Laurie; also a bundle of papers, which I receive very regularly. It is so very good of you all to write such lovely letters and I would dearly love to send each of you a long one in return, but I cannot, for both time and restrictions re the amount of our letters will not permit it. Therefore I must write a short one to you collectively, but you must each treat it as if 'twas written to you individually also.

In the first place all I can say about my doings of late is that we are doing our bit right enough and it is not always pleasant either. But our battalion has suffered less than any other in the division and my own particular section has not yet had a casualty, and we are always well up in the Front Line, too! May our luck continue always, eh?

I had a new experience the other night; a reconnaissance among the ice and snow of 'No Man's Land', in the company of half-a-dozen others. It was very interesting, but beastly cold and we returned without any interference from Fritz.

Your loving and interesting letters are read over and over, you bet, and I am pleased to note that you are all well, and that things generally are jogging along pretty well. You will understand that I can but make few comments on the many, many interesting passages that all your letters contain. You must not, any of you, be hurt if I refer to only one or two, will you?

By the way, I was surprised to hear that Palmers are removing to Jamestown. I s'pose a change of surroundings is their reason, since poor old Alan will never return. So glad you're off for a trip, Bert and Ron. I'll look forward to a record of your doings Bert. You are a dear to write every mail. I love to hear all about what takes place in your little home

Same to you, Fred and Evelyn, George and Con. Tell us all about the kiddies. I like to hear of their pranks and sayings. They are dear kids. I do hope dear Con that you are well and strong and that everything is O.K. <u>Do you get me</u>?

Gee! There must have been some crowd at the fete. I should like to have been there with you.

You <u>are</u> getting grown up 'Young Un'. I guess you will enjoy the pen painting. Fancy you travelling to and fro on the cars all alone. You will sure be a big girl by the time I return.

As usual Bert, Mill, Mother and Dad, your letters were all that could be desired. No doubt you will realise by your own eagerness for letters how we boys look forward to mail days. Mail days and paydays are the 'red-letter' days for us!

Feb.3rd, 1917

My work lately has been away from the section so that I have seen very little of Bert. You will judge of my surprise and anxiety when I learnt last night that Bert had been taken to the hospital in the afternoon suffering from influenza or something like that. I believe I was hoping to be able to see him today but cannot and don't know when I shall be able to.

I do hope the poor old kid is not very bad. He was asking for me, too, I believe! Still, even slight cases of sickness have to be treated at the hospital. As Bert was pretty right when I saw him only a day or two ago, I'm hoping to see him back with us very soon. 'Tis of no use me dropping a line to his people for I don't really know what is wrong with him and may cause them unnecessary anxiety.

I must close now or I may be hauled over the coals for writing too long a letter. Our O.C. is a bonza chap and gives us a better deal regarding our letters than the company men receive, so we must not spoil a good thing.

Once again I assure you I have never felt so fit as I am now, despite the intense cold.

With heaps of love and kisses to each one of you I'll say *Au Revoir*.

Yours very lovingly,
"Theo"

Fred and Evelyn, your letters were a bit delayed and were a pleasant surprise and very interesting – keep on doing it, won't you.

Somewhere In France.
Feb.11th, 1917
My dearest Homefolks,

A few days ago I received a budget of letters from all of you, also that lovely big parcel, for which I thank you. The contents of the parcel were delightful and gave pleasure to my mates as well as myself. Especially those homemade sweets which were a great delicacy and they disappeared with astonishing rapidity. You should have seen the boys jump when I asked them to try some home-made sweets from Australia.

The tobacco, cigarettes and pipe also were A.1. (I had broken my pipe only a couple of days previously, so the new one came at the right time, eh?) All the other numerous things were just the thing, and please, you dears, accept my very heartiest loving thanks for your goodness in taking so much trouble over the same.

The same to you dear Gawler folk.[81] I am quite looking forward to getting the parcel, which you so lovingly prepared and forwarded. Altho' I have not yet received it, I may get it any time now.

The news that Aunt Jane is going to live with you did not come as a very great surprise, but I'm afraid it will mean a lot more work for you, Mother-mine. Could you use some of my money in the way of getting assistance? You know, I don't want you to go knocking yourself up! How about considering it? But don't think about it too long, you know!

With regard to myself, I haven't much to relate. Things get pretty lively at times, but so far I am enjoying things as far as possible. I am in the very best of health and spirits.

A little over a week ago two of our gunners were slightly wounded by shrapnel. One of them (Harry Cook from Mt. Barker) is back again quite alright. But it will be some little time before the other chap is with us again, I think.

It has been beastly cold, but the last few days Old Sol has been exerting his influence a bit and made the atmosphere a trifle warmer, thank goodness.

I can picture you dear ones writing your Xmas letters to me. You will have known before you receive this how we spent Xmas over here and that my thoughts were with you all

The parcels which I receive are always crammed full and 'tis always a source of wonder to me how you manage to get so many goodies into the space available.

By the way, I am pleased to hear of Phil H's[82] success. So far I have received no letter from her this mail, and she had not missed a mail. I intend thanking them for contributions to the parcel.

I hope you enjoyed the visit to Gawler, Mother, Laurie, Bert and kiddies – guess you'd have a good time. Also I do

81 Theo's sister Constance, who married George Hicks, lived in Gawler

82 Female cousin

hope the transit of Aunt Jane from the Mount to our home was accomplished successfully. It would, sure, be a big undertaking.

Your news re our battalion being in France was quite right, Dad. We are quite old warriors now.

I do hope that your good run will long continue and that you will keep in excellent health. It will be A.1. to be building near home. It makes a long day of it when you have any distance to go, doesn't it?

It is good to hear poor old Alan highly praised; he was a dear old lad, and I'm very glad to hear that he was so successful as an officer.

Yours was a bonnie long letter, dear Dad! I hope you have a good time at Pinnaroo. You remember me telling you in my last letter that Bert W. had gone into hospital. Well, until yesterday I could hear very little about him. However I received a note from him saying that he was having a few days rest after a slight touch of rheumatic fever and would be with us again in a day or two. So that's alright, isn't it?

By the way the Vancouver mail and Xmas mail reached me together. As far as I remember, my cable to you cost 6/-. (Special rate for troops!)

So Millie and Laurie are still as lively as crickets. Wait till I get back, and then won't we have some gay times!! You bet we do look forward to the time when our job is done and we can get back home – 'HOME'. How good that little word sounds!

I'm thinking I must close now.

With all good wishes and many thanks for loving letters and parcels and very fondest love and heaps of kisses to each one of you – Mother, Father, Sisters and Brothers –
From
Yours Lovingly,
"Theo"

Monday, February 19th 1917.[83]

Made a raid on German trenches aided by a heavier barrage of artillery than even the Somme has seen. Out of 62 who went over 36 were casualties (2 killed). Altho' many were wounded before they got into the trenches they kept on, killing a few 'squareheads', and secured the required information afterwards returning to our own lines in excellent order and without haste, bringing back all wounded. I was in charge of a machine gun with a gunner and two bombers out in No Man's Land near Fritz's lines covering the left flank of the party. It was hell let loose right enough and Fritz's lines were ablaze with the bursting of high explosions and shrapnel and pieces of wire flying everywhere. Our boys were wonderful and I was proud to be with the party; but I should have liked to have gone right in: however our job was to stay outside and stop any flanking movement by Fritz.

Somewhere in France
Feb.22nd, 1917

My dearest Homefolks,
You will remember in a letter that I wrote you some time ago that a number of men from our battalion were in training for a special job. Well, that training was continued at intervals until last Monday night, the 19th, when we made an attempt to carry out the work that had been allotted to us. This was to make a raid on Fritz's[84] trenches on a certain point in our sector.

The other battalions of the brigade had made their raids but had met with little or no success. Ours was the last battalion to carry out its stunt. We had put in some good training in football and physical exercises to make us fit. In fact that constituted

---

83 Theo's diary entries start here and are spasmodic.

84 German army

most of our training, combined with revolver shooting, bombing and bayonet fighting for those who had been selected for such work.

We all had a turn at different times, having a look over No Man's Land, so as to get the lay of the land.

Last Sunday night a party of us (5 N.C.O.s and an officer) went over the sector where the raid was made in order that Archie Fletcher and I should be sure of our gun positions for the night of the raid.

It was very dark and enemy machine guns were popping, and to some purpose, too, for another patrol on our right suffered, one officer being killed. However, the guns were playing on our flanks and we were not troubled. After finding out what we wanted, we returned in safety.

The following night was the night. Before we set out the Brigadier and Major Butler addressed us. We were promised a heavier barrage of artillery to aid us than had even been witnessed on the Somme. All arrangements were perfect and at the appointed time over the top we went led by our scouts.

Everything went well. Our party got through our own wires and to a point about 20 yards from Fritz's parapet. I went to the left with my gun, one gunner and two bombers. While I was getting them places in shell holes, bullets were whistling unpleasantly close from an enemy gun over on the right, but they didn't touch us.

We no sooner got settled in our position than our artillery opened fire and soon the enemy's Front Line was all-ablaze with bursting shells of every description. The air was full of flying shrapnel and bits of shell. Talk about a 'Fifth of November'[85] or 'hell let loose' – they were not in the same street!

'Tis hard to give you a conception of what really did take

---

85 November 5th 1605, the night when Guy Fawkes was captured and the Gun Powder plot was thwarted against King James I of England. This was celebrated every year on this date.

place. Smoke was rolling from the German trenches in clouds. This could be seen by the light of rockets (or Verie[86] Lights as they are called) which Fritz was sending up in great numbers, making everything as bright as day. The barrage on his Front Line lasted for a few minutes then lifted back into his supports. Our chaps rushed forward from the point where they had assembled and went right over into Fritz's trench.

I say trench, but our artillery bombardment had changed it from a trench into a series of shell-holes. It must have blown to pieces any of the enemy who had previously manned it. Some were found dead; our chaps killed a few as they proceeded along the trench. The party came to a large dugout over which it seems two Germans stood on guard. One was bayoneted and the other fled inside barring the entrance of our chaps by closing a huge steel door.

A small party had been provided with explosives to deal with such obstacles, but as ill luck would have it, all of these were casualties and our chaps were doomed to disappointment. By no other way could they get in but by blowing open the door. The raid was a success and the raiders received the praise of the 'heads' of the brigade and the division for the useful information, which they were able to obtain.

You will be wondering what I was doing all this time. Well, Archie Fletcher and I were in charge of a machine gun on either flank out in No Man's Land near Fritz's wires. Our job was to lie quiet and cut into any party of the enemy, which might try to outflank our comrades. This was rather a cold-footed job in comparison to what the others went through, but nevertheless we had our share.

The positions where we were in readiness received due attention and there was more shrapnel, high explosives, etc., than was at all comfortable; not to mention the fact that we were waist-deep in mud and water for a couple of hours or so.

86 Magic Lights – this is how open fire was seen by the troops at night.

We remained out there till all our chaps were in and we knew by previous orders when to move.

Everything was comparatively quiet as we moved back to our own trench, and it was very dark. We had a shallow creek to cross on the way and when wading through this we heard men moving somewhere in the darkness on the other side. Having crossed we moved slowly along, well on the alert; then in the darkness we saw half a dozen forms moving towards us. With revolvers ready we challenged them.

We were greatly relieved to find they were our own scouts.

Continuing on we got safely in through our own wires and over the parapet. Up to that time we were entirely in the dark as to how the chaps had fared. On enquiry we learned that they had made a good job of it but had not escaped scatheless.

One of those who were wounded was Lieut. Price, a fine fellow and one whom we all liked immensely. Those who were casualties were helped back by their mates. One or two will never fight again, I'm sorry to say.

Everything was done in excellent order and many brave deeds were performed. No doubt you will read shortly that a few of the boys have won some distinction or other. When you take into consideration the fact that No Man's Land is a network of shell holes and the parts not so touched up form a veritable bog, you will understand what the boys did on Monday night. Our officers cannot say enough in praise of the way the raiders did their job and got back their wounded. I was proud to be one of the number, even though I did not have a chance to hop in and 'get my cut!' Anyway, we did our job. Mr Cope said he could not understand how Archie's and my parties escaped without a casualty. I guess our good angel was in attendance, eh?

I'm afraid the censor won't appreciate a long epistle. So I must close for this time assuring you of my excellent health and spirits, and trusting that all you dear ones at home are A.1. too.

With fondest love to you all and also to Aunt Jane, I'll say *Au Revoir* for this time.
Your loving Son and Brother,
"Theo"

Somewhere in France
9.3.17

My dearest Homefolks,
In writing the date I just remember that we have been away from dear old South Aus. For nine months today. And what a lot has been crammed into that time.

Still, it has been a pretty happy time and strenuous too. But I'm jolly glad I'm having the experience. Nevertheless, I hope it won't be long now before we return to our own land once again. Then won't we have some jolly times?

A couple of mails came in within a few days this time and I have had a very big bundle of letters from you all and from Ivey. I'm sure glad that you were able to get Aunt Jane through that journey safe and sound and that she is happy in our home.

I cannot reply to queries this time for I am running close to the mail closing and have to be satisfied with a short note to you. Old Fritz has not caught Bert or me yet but things get pretty lively at times.

This March weather is bitterly cold with winds that go straight through one, and make a chap want some of the sunshine of his own country. However, it could be a jolly sight worse, I s'pose, and with plenty of food and good clothing we fare alright.

Please accept my congrats. Con and George. I hope everyone, including the young 'un (whose acquaintance I hope to make in the near future) are all O.K.

By the way, Mother, I was talking to a chap in one of the Queensland battalions the other day and during the conversation it transpired that he knew you. He's an old S.A. boy. Skewes by name, and he was at Osborne's Beach when you and Laurie were recuperating there some few years ago. He wished me to remember him to you. Do you remember?

So glad to hear that everything is O.K. at home, but sorry to know that you, Fred old boy, are off colour. I do hope you'll soon be right again.

Must close now; time presses. More anon.
Fondest love,
"Theo"

Friday, March 9th 1917.
Up before the Brigadier with reference to being sent to a training school.

Evening:
Had to attend at Battalion headquarters re same to give certain particulars. Recommendation fixed up and I expect to go to the school within a couple of weeks. Had a day off from the trenches and spent an idle day. Met Allan Battye (11th A.M.C.) in the evening – first since we were in Lark Hill – I enjoyed a nice chat. He wished me to thank Millie for the Xmas card she sent him. Having another spell – writing letters, etc.

Monday, March 12th 1917
We left our billets at Amentieres in the afternoon and marched to the ruined village of Le Bizet where we billeted for the night. Had a good night's rest in someone's home – or the remains of it.

Tuesday, March 13th 1917
Went into the new sector of Le Bizet where we spent the night at an old farmhouse. Here we had the best quarters of any that

has fallen to our share, but 'twas only for the night, for next morning we were on the move again.

Wednesday, March 14th 1917.
Up and away early in charge of 10 men and made our way to a certain redouter[87] where the company's quarters were situated. From here we took turns with another gun team in putting in 24 hours in the Front Line. To-night it's our turn to spend a good night here in comparative comfort.

Thursday, March 15th 1917.
We have relieved our comrades and find that there is not much shelter from the weather here. Water, which is knee deep, lies in the trench on each side of us. 24 hours continuously on the alert is quite enough for such a 'joint' as this.

Friday, March 16th 1917.
About narrowest escape yet. I was on sentry and a Fritz must have seen me for a bullet knocked into pieces the sandbag alongside my right ear. A gunman and I then carried on a rifle duel with our friend opposite and he called out to us twice, whether in derision or not I cannot say.

Saturday, March 17th 1917 – St Patrick's Day
Today is sunny with a brisk breeze. Aeroplanes on both sides are active and we saw one of ours bought down in flames by Fritz – damn him!

Sunday, March 18th 1917 – 4th Sunday in Lent
Started morning sniping at Fritz who put up a white flag and kept it there 'till evening. Saw two heads wearing spiked helmets.

---

87 Redout – trenches with sandbags outside or within a fortification

Monday, March 19th 1917
Spent day in position behind Front Line; had a shave and a sleep and in the afternoon moved back into a ruined village where we were to billet for a few days while doing repair work.

Tuesday, March 20th 1917
Spent the morning at the divisional baths having a clean up. In the afternoon. enjoyed a nice sing-song at our soldiers club – in an old house, where a piano and a warm fire added to our enjoyment. Received a bonza parcel from home. Best of all – 'tis pay day. So being provided with a few francs we walked into the adjacent village of Pont de Nieppe where we had a bonza feed of eggs and chips. While there one of Fritz's shells burst in the town killing 5 Tommies, a French soldier just arrived on long leave after 2 years service, and the soldier's mother.

Thursday, March 22nd, 1917
Each day since coming away from the Front Line we have been cleaning out drains and the weather has been very severe – wind, rain, sleet and snow. This morning Fritz shelled us out of it – bad luck to him. Spent the evening writing letters to the Homefolks, Ivey and Phil. The snow fell very heavily in the evening.

<u>Somewhere in Belgium</u>
March 23rd, 1917

My dearest Homefolks,
Many thanks for the bonza parcel which I received from you on the 20th containing an assortment of delicacies which I greatly appreciate. You bet I look forward to receiving the parcels from home. And now I am eagerly waiting for letters which, as usual, we are expecting every day. But they seem long in coming.

Mail days, you know, are the best days – the only complaint is that they don't come often enough! But when they do come and I get all the bonnie letters and loving messages from you all, it seems worthwhile.

This month is the most trying one, I think – plenty of wind, snow, rain and a mixture of the lot. But that doesn't make any difference to our job. We have to get out into it just the same. The snow is falling in one white cloud now and makes me feel glad that my work for today is finished. I started out in the early hours and came back at dinnertime. Others have to go out now and work part of the night – poor beggars!

We get our share during the day, but it's worse for the night parties. I guess Dad knows what it is like out in the open in such weather.

Isn't it great to read of the way our side is moving at present on some of the fronts. Makes us wish that our time to go ahead had arrived at last. We have been in touch with the New Zealanders lately. They are great fellows and dashed good fighters.

I'm writing this in someone's ruined home which has been utilised as a Soldier's Club, with books and papers, writing tables and a <u>piano</u>. Quite a lot to be thankful for, eh? Some of the boys get around the piano of a night and we have a good old singsong. Can't you picture us? Reminds me of the good old times at home! It's jolly cold, though.

Some little time ago my gun team took the opportunity of having our photos taken. So far our ranks are unbroken, altho' a while ago one of Fritz's minnies[88] blew up the position which the team occupied, partially burying Tom Potticary and shaking the others up. Fred Sharman and Co. were at the raiding school then. I haven't enough P.C.s[89] to go around, so I am enclosing

---

88 'Minnie' was a term used to describe the German trench mortar minniewerfer

89 Post Cards

one each for Father and Mother. <u>Perhaps</u> I'll have one of myself to send to you all later on.

I tried to get some birthday cards to send to you 'April kids' but couldn't find any. In looking around for them I was too late even to write you all my good wishes. So, altho' rather late in coming, will you accept my very best wishes and love Bertha, Fred, Daisy, Millie and Laurie, and you too, George? (Connie evidently thought there were not enough birthdays in April amongst us, so she brought in another, eh?)[90]

It was rather funny the other day. We had just been ploughing through mud and slush to reach a farm where we spent the night. The first thing that we saw when entering the door was 'Smile, damn you, smile!' which some wag had written up on the wall. So, of course, we smiled. We couldn't help it!

I'm glad that you all received my Xmas greetings alright. Sorry, Fred, old man, that you had such a rough time at Xmas, but trust that you are A.1. now. I received your newsy letter of 7th January, old boy, and I wouldn't mind having a bit of the weather, which you spoke of, just as a change from rain, snow and mud. So, Charl. Perryman is having his second cut. Good on his pluck! This will be a change after Gallipoli, I reckon.

Say, Mother, I didn't know when writing to Harvey and Auntie Liz that <u>you</u> would be at the Mount to read them. I'm jolly glad it was so, as the one I wrote would not reach you for a day or two. You must have had an awfully strenuous time at the Mount, arranging for poor old Auntie's conveyance to town, Mother-mine, and I hope it did not have a bad effect on your health. How is Auntie enjoying her new surroundings?

I am rereading your letter, Bert and I am nearly frozen. It's good weather here for freezing purposes, but not for eating ice-creams! I'm glad that you, your hubby and the pigeon pair are O.K.

---

90 Surprisingly all the siblings mentioned were born in April.

No, Laurie, Bert Westeley was not included in the photo group which I sent you all for Xmas. One of the boys came in with his camera and snapped a few of us who were seated round the stove reading and writing.

How are you and the new arrival getting on, Con? How are Curly and Fat? I don't suppose you will have much time for writing now, but write as often as you can, won't you? Perhaps there are letters from all of you not far away. I hope so. How are the eyes, George?[91] Quite alright now, I hope.

Bert told me in her letter, Dad, that you were looking splendid and I'm glad it is so, and I hope the biz[92] is good.

You all tell me to look after myself. You just bet I do my best in that direction. And mind you look after yourselves, too, because I want to see you all looking tip-top when I get back home again.

Now I must say *Au Revoir* once again.

With love and kisses to each one of you from

Your Loving Son and Bro.

"Theo"

Friday, March 23rd, 1917

On the drains again this morning. So far no snow has fallen but it is exceedingly cold. Fritz just put a couple of shells where we are working and scattered us – again without results. Went to QMS[93] for new tunic, breeches and hat and was only successful in getting the last named.

---

91 Connie's husband

92 business

93 Quarter Master Store – army supplies

Saturday, March 24th 1917
No fatigue for specialists; supposed to go into Front Line, but 'twas postponed. Was sent up into trenches with a fatigue party – very cold indeed. Didn't get back to billets until late. Got the doctor to sign insurance paper.

Sunday, March 25th 1917.
Stood by for trenches all day – cancelled again. Went to Church Service at the Club. Had a very enjoyable time.

Monday, March 26th 1917.
Again stood by for the trenches and some went in. Together with 3 others, I was paraded before the Colonel, who said that very shortly I would be sent to a training school as I had been recommended for a commission. Good News, eh what. Went down to the village and while there saw a New Zealander leading his French bride away from the church.

Tuesday, March 27th 1917
Battalion came into the firing line this morning. Dressed to the accompaniment of the roar of the artillery and machine guns on Fritz, who was making an unsuccessful attempt to push back the N.Z.s on our left. Took over the front trenches and the day and night passed very quietly indeed.

Wednesday, March 28th 1917
Fired 10 mags last night – 500 rounds. Slept from 6 to 12 this morning. Bert W. who is attached to the Lewis Gun Officers at headquarters was around at dinnertime. Fritz sent over a few shells this morning, but not many. Later on he sent over minnies not far away from our position, sending one of the gun teams packing. No one hurt.

Thursday, March 29th 1917
Last night it was bitterly cold and pitch dark with a driving rain

and altogether a miserable combination. Did very little firing;
about 4 magazines. The same weather conditions, without the
wind continued to-day and makes life in the Front Line very
unpleasant; added to this Fritz has been sending over more
'minnies' and 'pineapples' in return for 'plum puddings' sent
over by our chaps. Fired 5 mags. last night.

Friday, March 30th 1917.
Usual standing to.[94] *Very little sleep. Fired 10 mags. Last*
night.

Somewhere in Belgium
March 30th, 1917

My dearest Homefolks,
Bert W. has brought me news that mail closes for home in a day
or two so I must start right away and write you a few lines.

In the first place, Mother dear, I must thank you for sending
along that insurance paper to be filled in and which I have
fixed up but forgot to enclose in my last letter. Circumstances
prevented me from seeing to it before. I hope it is not too late,
but the conditions, which we are under, are to blame for the
delay. I hope the AMP will take that in consideration.

Our mail from home is long overdue owing to enemy action.
It seems quite a long time since we last received any letters and
we call Fritz all sorts of names for stopping it for us. I believe
a mail or two back, one of our mails from here went down, but
whether 'tis true or not, I cannot say – hope it was not so.

We are having a pretty dreary time in the line this time for
the weather is pretty boisterous. By Jove, we will be jolly glad
when the fine weather comes! In our sector of the line we are
only 50 yards from the German lines, so of course we have to
keep a keen look out. Altho' we are so close to Fritz we have

---

94 Standing at the ready in case of an attack

our intervals of sleep, you bet. But if that gentleman paid us a visit, those 'off shift' would be out of the dug-out in no time to have their cut at Fritz.

The last couple of afternoons Fritz has strafed us with various explosives and torn the trenches about some, but luckily no casualties were inflicted. Of course he did not have all the say for he generally gets more in return from our artillery, etc. At this game I can assure you we quite believe in the old saying that, 'It is better to give than to receive!' However, it is truly marvellous what an immense amount of explosives can be thrown into a sector and yet no casualties result there from. It may be that ours is a particularly lucky battalion!

Do you know, I was with you all at home in my dreams this morning. It was grand to be home again, but it was a sudden return to reality when I was awakened to take my turn during the cold, dark two hours before daylight, with a heavy fall of rain to add to the enjoyment.

I must leave off for a few minutes for our chaps are going to strafe Fritz and I guess things will be a bit lively for a time.

(Later)
We were given to understand that there was to be some strafe. But nothing much happened.

I have been recommended to go to a training school, which recommendation has been approved of. I expect to go away for this purpose shortly to a place away from the firing line. If I am successful it will mean promotion for me. Nevertheless it will be a hard row to hoe, as I have not been through any infantry training schools. But I intend to do my best and hope to prove successful. The Colonel could not say when I'm likely to go.

News is scarce. I'm as well as ever and enjoying this life. I sincerely trust that you are all in good health and spirits also. *Au Revoir*, dear ones.
Fondest love and kisses from yr. loving Son and Brother,
"Theo"

Saturday, March 31st 1917
Ditto. Snow, sleet and wind. Rotten weather. Fired 6 mags.

Saturday, March 31st, 1917
I have just received some lovely letters from Mother, Dad, Bert, Mill, Laurie and Phil, dated on or about Jan. 14th. Many thanks all of you for congrats re promotion. I'm so glad to hear that things are going well with you all and trust that they will long continue so. No time to reply to queries, etc.,
Fondest love to all and to Aunt Jane,
from, yours lovingly,
"Theo"

Sunday April 1st 1917.
Nasty cold night. At 4.25 a.m. a party of Germans got into the line and came towards our gun. Drove them away; no one injured.

Friday, April 6th 1917. Good Friday
Left L. B. sector. Had a good feed and went to the Military Cinema. Sort of celebrating.

Monday, April 9th 1917. Easter Monday
Lent F.W, 5 francs. Wrote to Sr. Osborne.

Somewhere in Belgium
April 12, 1917

My dearest Mother,
Before I forget. In his letter to me recently my old O.C. Lieut. Osborne, (who is being invalided back to S.A.) asked if he could do anything for me when he got to the other side. So when answering I asked him if he would be so kind, sometime when he was at leisure, as to call on my homefolk and tell you I'm getting on A.1.

I thought, as he has been with us for so long and knows what we have been up to, and was with us for some time in the trenches, he would be able to give you some first hand information. He is a dear old chap, just like a father to us. I'm sure he won't mind doing that much for me. I know that you will give him a royal welcome.

You see, I am taking it for granted that he will do the favour I ask of him. But he's such a bonza old chap that I know he will. So if Lieut. Osborne comes looking you up, you will know it is because I asked him to. Capt. Stewart knows him well.

I have a much better chance to write this week for instead of going out on fatigue work I have been given the job of overhauling the battalion's guns and gear. So I feel better fit for writing of an evening. I've rigged up a bench in a stable and things look quite businesslike, I can assure you. My bed is on a heap of straw in the corner. After many efforts and a great deal of smoke, I have succeeded in getting a good fire going. I tell you, things look quite comfy.

You will know long ere this, Mother-mine, that I have made out fresh allotment papers; the matter was delayed a lot, but it was not the fault of the battalion clerks – no papers were available. It is good to know that you have no trouble in getting my money. I don't anticipate any necessity for cabling for money, but should I do so, the inclusion on the name of Dad's native town will convince you that it is dinkum.

I expect I'll be getting those later parcels that you mention very soon. We get 'em all in the long run.

The knowledge that all you dear ones are praying for us helps wonderfully, Mother-mine. I know that you believe in telepathy and I do hope that you can <u>feel</u> that I am <u>well</u>, <u>strong</u> and <u>happy</u>. I don't forget to pray for you dear ones at home and I trust that we will soon succeed in pushing our enemies so hard that they will give in, and then we can come back home again. Gee! Won't that be alright? I'm afraid I do a great deal of air castle[95] building, but what matter?

Poor little Laurie, I'm so very, very sorry to hear that she is still so badly troubled with that nasty complaint. Also about Fred. It's about time they took him away from that Strath. P.M.[96] – he's a _____ Rotter!

I had to laugh when you mentioned how I used to worry about my pulse. I haven't forgotten it. What a little fool I was!

Poor Mother, I do wish you could have a better time of it. I'm jolly glad, though, that you have been able to obtain the services of a good girl – even if she is so deaf!

So, Nature is turning things topsy-turvy too. I hope she doesn't make too many changes in the flowers and vegetables though, before I get back, or I shall wonder what kind of a country I have returned to.

I'm so glad that you were pleased with my attempt at keeping a diary, but you praise it too highly, dear. I have not written up any since because things are pretty much of a muchness. Also it would not do to be found with such in my possession.

I look at it this way, I do my best to keep you well posted up in my letters as to my experiences; also there are many things in this game that it would be far better to forget than to bring back to one's mind in the days to come. I think my memory is capable of retaining sufficient material for many a fireside yarn when I get back to you.

No, Mother dear, your letters are not censored. You speak disparagingly of your letters and you <u>should</u> <u>not</u>, for they are just lovely. It is good to be a 'soldier boy' if 'tis only to receive the beautiful letters which my loved ones and my friends write to me. I should like to be able to keep them, but of course

---

95 Building castles in the air – or dreaming of the future

96 Fred's employer was the Strathalbyn Post Master

I cannot, and must do the next best thing – keep the loving contents in my memory.

A mail closes tomorrow and another a couple of days later, so I am endeavouring to write to you all individually this time and trust that nothing will eventuate to prevent it. So much for this time.

Au Revoir, Mother-mine. Don't worry about me, dear, for I am A.1. and enjoying life.

Fondest love and kisses from

Your loving Son,

"Theo"

Somewhere in Belgium
April 12th, 1917

My dearest Dad,

I am pleased beyond measure, as you know, to receive your letters and to know that both your health and your work are keeping satisfactory. Many thanks for your congrats re securing my second stripe; I too hope that it won't be long before I advance a bit higher.

Yes, we were well equipped for our work over here, and that stood us in good stead for the winter. Altho' it has been pretty severe, we are warmly clothed and well fed and have stood it well in spite of its severity and our being unaccustomed to the intense cold. You bet we felt it pretty badly and wondered how we would get through some of the nights, but we have all come out smiling.

Every day when we are in the trenches we have a change of socks issued, and about every week or two we go to the divisional baths for a good hot bath and an entire change of underclothing. So you see, if a fellow looks after himself he has a pretty good chance of keeping well and fit. I have been in splendid health right through – not even a cold to trouble me since that one which I brought over from England and lost here. It will be 'some experience' won't it, if I can get through the 'big push' alright and come back to you all again to tell you all about it. And I'm coming back – never fear!

What think you of America coming into the mix, Dad? They ought to make a big difference in our favour. I hope they'll prove as good hustlers at the war game as they are at piling up the dollars, and won't spend too much time in talking about it.

I'm glad you have sold the Mount block at a satisfactory figure and trust that you will have been successful in advantageously disposing of Aunt Jane's property. I appreciate your trust in taking me into your confidence with regard to some important matters and I consider it only just that such should be the case with respect to that particular matter. Do you get me?

I know that you will all be worrying a great deal about me in these times when our side is pushing forward. But don't worry too much – I've had just a few close calls since we've been over here, and I am quite convinced that I am destined to return safely to you. Anyway, I've tried to play the game right through and will continue to do so.

You will have read in a previous letter that my team was transferred a while back to 'B.' Coy.; well Capt. Harry Cope is our O.C., and Lieut. Will Shanasy my platoon officer. (Millie will remember the latter if you cannot recall him; he used to go to school when we did). Sad to relate though, Mr. Shanasy was badly wounded about a week ago. He was inspecting that part of the line where one of Fritz's minniewerfus blew in the part of the line where my gun was placed. When a German sniper got him, the bullet laying open one side of his face. The wound was a horrible one, but I believe Mr. Shanasy is getting along pretty well. He was an excellent officer and one of the best of fellows and everyone is grieved to lose him. Still, 'tis the fortune of war, I suppose.

Well, dear Dad, I must say *Au Revoir* for this time, and try

and write a note at least to each of the others if I can. So with fondest love and best of wishes I'll say ta! ta!
Your Loving Son,
"Theo"

Somewhere in France
May 10th, 1917

My dearest Homefolks,
Letters from you all arrived last evening and of course brought joy in their train. We always get a bit impatient and worry the clerks if the mail is a day or two overdue. But when the letters do come, happiness reigns again. But like you, no sooner have I read my letters than I am counting the days and longing for the next batch.

We are lucky chaps in as much as we are out of sound of the roar of the guns and have a short respite from trench life. It took a strenuous march of a few days to bring us to our present location, and as La Belle France is once again clothing herself in a mantle of beauty, our journey here was a not an unpleasant experience. Each night we billeted in some farmer's barns, where a plentiful supply of straw provided us with quite a luxurious couch. Always there was a plentiful supply of water to bathe and refresh ourselves after the long march, and of course after such a day, one did not need any rocking to induce sleep.

Each morning the camp was very early astir and an early start was made, so that our next stop was reached soon after mid-day. If near a town we had a few hours to look around, or else to rest. The march was a test of efficiency and endurance and all the battalions of the brigade took part, and I am pleased to say that our battalion finished up with the best record.

While in our present billets, although we are enjoying a

spell from the Front Line, we are not idle, but continue training to keep us fit. I got through the marching alright, but a couple of days after our arrival I developed a sore heel, which the doc. describes as a septic heel. It has been a bit sore and has necessitated my remaining behind for a rest while the others go out to work. I don't like it at all, for I should be with them gaining experience. Never mind, I'll be with them tomorrow, I think, for my foot is much better today. With the exception of the foot, I'm as right as a trivet.

This time I received letters from, Mother, Dad, Mill and Laurie, that is, from you folks at home; also, of course, from Ivey, Phil, Jean Badger and Mill Clark. Not so bad, eh?

Yes, Dad, I weathered the severe winter very well and no shell or bullet has yet had my number on it, and, like 'Johnny Walker' I'm 'still going strong'– stronger in fact! I read with interest, always, your views on things political and agree with you in many things.

Your news, Mother and Dad that the increase in my allotments has been paid to you is very satisfactory. It takes such a long time for answers to letters to be received and I have often wondered if the fresh papers I made out had reached the authorities alright. It is good to know the matter has been fixed up without any difficulty. I hope the insurance matter will be fixed up in a like manner, despite the unavoidable delay.

I seem to be lucky with regard to the parcels you send, all of which appear to reach me ultimately. Early last month I received a tin of goodies and about the 28th of April I received a tin from the Mount containing a large cake, several packets of biscuits and various sweets, evidently the one that you had arranged with Auntie Liz to send on. You bet the boys of my team and I enjoyed the contents – thanks so very, very much dear ones, for your great kindness in sending these.

It was rather a pity, wasn't it, Dad, that you could not go

either to Pinnaroo or Woodside, but circumstances of course would not permit it.

When I read in your last letter that Phil had received a letter, and neither you nor Ivey's had come to light, I recognised that it would appear odd, but I reckoned that you all would know that there was sure to be others somewhere and that you would not jump to wrong conclusions; I'm glad that I was right – in your case at least, Mother dear.

You bet, I was delighted to receive that cablegram. You would once again be able to say, 'I told you so', wouldn't you, Mother? You shouldn't worry so much about the parcels, Mother dear, I have received lots, all that you have sent, I believe, and I always notify you with regard to them. The parcels always arrive some little time after letters, which are not to be surprised at considering the enormous amount of letters and parcels that have to be handled.

I am glad to hear that Aunt Jane is keeping fairly well, considering everything; please give her my love. 'Tis good to hear that Laurie is able to help you so much; that is a good criterion that her health must be improving. The trouble with your leg and knee must have greatly troubled you, Mother dear, but I am so very glad to know that all's well once again.

So the postal authorities have at last seen fit to give you a spell, Fred; and 'tis to be hoped that you won't have to return to duty under the Strath. P.M. again. I shall be looking forward to receiving a long letter soon telling of your doings. By the letter just received, you had two or three from me at the time of writing. It's rather aggravating when they come like that, isn't it, in as much as the interval either before or until the next mail must of necessity be a long one.

As usual yours was a bonnie little letter Laurie dear. It was rather unfortunate that it should rain on the day the Roll of Honour was unveiled. So you have been enjoying yourself with Rea, Betty and Glen. Poor little Betty, I hope she hasn't been ill since you wrote. 'Tis rather peculiar that she should get those giddy turns. I hope you are keeping well and strong, dear girl

I haven't been able to write the extra letters to you yet, Con and George, Dais and Ted, but hope to soon. By the way, haven't you bush farming people an interval to spare to drop a few lines this way. How about having a try? It would be appreciated.

I say, Mill, you must surely be in love, for you forgot to complete your letter this time, breaking off at page 3; when you were speaking of one, Clinton Tucker, whom I <u>don't</u> remember. By the way, Mill, there's one young fellow whom I would like to hear about, and in connection with whom you are very reticent. Is it a serious affair this time, Mill? If the young chap towards whom I am making these references has succeeded in awaking <u>your</u> lively interest, he must be one of extra special quality. Now, don't get cross, Mill; if I was home you know I'd be sure to tease, and altho' I am so far away I still avail myself of that brotherly privilege. I guess those pictures of London, which you saw, must have been taken in pre-war days, for London as we saw it was not so greatly crowded, and at night owing to the Zepp. menace, the streets were almost in darkness. Could you imagine Bert and I roaming around those historic places?

Bert has at last been given his long promised third stripe and is now Sergt. Westley. I see very little of Bert nowadays for his work does not allow of it.

It must be *Au Revoir* now for this time, dear ones. I didn't expect to manage a letter nearly as long as this – but here it is; and I hope it will interest you and help you to know that I'm O.K. in health and spirits and looking forward to the time when we are going to smash Kaiser Bill's troops and then go marching home.

So, ta! ta! with fondest love and heaps of kisses to each and every one, from,

Your loving Son and Brother,
"Theo"
P.S. I missed your usual bright and loving letters, Bert and
Con., but perhaps they will get here yet, - T.W.

Somewhere in France
May 13th, 1917

Dear Coz Frank and Nell.
Some little time back I received newsy letters from you both
and as we have been very busy since that time, this is about the
first opportunity of replying. You seem to take it for granted
that I write budgets of news to Ivey, but believe me, even she
has sometimes to be satisfied with a 'whizz-bang' (as the boys
have nicknamed the field cards). I always do my best to get a
letter away to the homefolks and 'the girl' each mail and then,
if opportunity offers, I write to the other corespondents.
    After five months of the trenches, I am still going strong
and have not received a scratch as yet, neither have I been sick
in spite of the specially severe winter which has just passed
away – and it was 'some' cold at times, I can assure you. Still,
there was one good thing about the intense cold, for the mud
and water kept frozen and hard and thus one of our greatest
discomforts was eliminated. At night, if sufficient fuel could be
begged, borrowed or pinched, we would have a fire to bring the
warmth back into our joints after a turn on watch. And keeping
watch on those winter nights was no joke, I can tell you, for
the intense cold, the snow and the sleet made things, anything
but pleasant. One feature for which we were devoutly thankful
during the winter nights was the hot drink, which was brought
to us every few hours, for which I believe we are indebted to
the various patriotic funds making such a thing possible. Can
you imagine anything better than a good hot drink of cocoa or
tea with, perhaps a dash of rum to add to its stimulating effect?
I can't.

Back in February a party from our battalion raided Fritz's lines, and I was in charge of a party of four, taking with us our little 'pop-gun'. Our artillery bombardment prior to our chaps hopping in was extremely heavy and searching and when our boys got into the lines, there was very little vestige of a trench left and only a few live Huns were encountered. Other Fritzs took cover in their shell proof dug-outs and the boys could not get at them for the Germans shelled their Front Line with shrapnel as our boys jumped in and it was here that most of our casualties occurred and our demolition party whose duty it was to blow an entrance to the above mentioned dug-outs was put out of action. However the raid was a success, in as much as valuable information was obtained, and that was our object. My party did not go into the trench but protected one of the flanks from a position near his lines. We were only waist deep in a shell hole filled with mud and water and there we remained for a couple of hours. We had an excellent view of the effect of our bombardment, for the enemy's lines were one mass of flame and smoke from bursting shells, and heavy smoke was rolling away for all the world like that resulting from a big bush fire. We were also in a good position to get plenty of curry from Fritz's guns and the air was humming with shrapnel and high explosive shells were dropping around, but none of us were hit. When our main party had returned safely it was our turn to move back and it was no light job to extricate ourselves from the mud hole, and weren't we cramped. On our return journey we had to cross a shallow creek and when about halfway over we heard a party moving in the darkness between ourselves and our own lines. Not knowing whether it was friend or foe we were ready for a 'box on'. We could dimly see them coming around us in a half-circle. One of my party rapped out a challenge and the answer made us feel greatly relieved, for it was a scouting party of our own. You bet we felt greatly relieved. We soon reached our own lines pretty well fatigued, where we learnt of success and also of the price, which had been paid for it. A few would not fight again and others received wounds more or less serious. That was my first exciting experience.

On two occasions the gun position of my team has been blown up. In the first instance, one chap was partially buried and the others pretty badly shaken. That occurred a couple of nights before the above raid and I of course, was away preparing for that stunt. Perhaps it was just as well, eh! On the second occasion my team was just giving to the rear for a rest, when another of Fritz's Minniewerfers blew up this other position. Again, neither the gun nor the team was injured.

Then, about six weeks ago a party of Fritzs paid my part of the line a visit. The night was a cold and windy one with an occasional fall of snow. About 4.30 a.m., when everything was calm and still, a cry rang out – 'Halt!' in a voice of startled surprise, followed by, 'Come on boys, into the ----s!' The call came from a couple of sentries a bit to our right. We rushed to their assistance, but were too late to get the Huns, who hared off as soon as the alarm was given. We opened fire with our little gun and three of us made off after them, but no sign of them could we see. They had evidently counted on silencing the sentry and getting on to my team. Questioning the sentry I learned that the Fritzs had come on to him very stealthily and when halted had sprung straight at him. The sentry's bayonet slid off a steel vest, which the Fritz wore and passed harmlessly over his shoulder and the German gripped our man by the throat and at the same time beat him over the head. The steel helmet lessened the effect of those blows and although the surprise gave the Hun an initial advantage, our man soon proved himself more than a match for his opponent. Everything occurred in a couple of seconds and as soon as our man tore Fritz's hold from his throat he gave us the alarm. Our other sentry had a go with his bayonet but as the trench was very narrow at this point he could not use it to the best advantage. Nevertheless the blood on his bayonet and blood marks left by the Fritzs in their flight showed that his efforts were not in vain. No sound of this silent struggle reached us and not until the sentry's cry went up did we know there was anything doing. Then of course the Huns cleared off in haste. Our luck was right out, wasn't it? The party evidently got into our lines through a gap and under cover of shell-craters and a ruined house. That's another one I owe Fritz when my chance comes. We got a German cap and some stick grenades out of the affair which Fritz had dropped in his haste to get out of our reach.

There are lots of things in my particular branch of fighting that make it exciting and interesting. Of course I have had quite a few close calls (who hasn't?), but my number is not up yet. Many a lively duel do we have with Fritz's gunners. It is a frequent occurrence for the sandbags all round one to be cut with machine gun bullets and yet for one not to get hit. One of my narrowest squeaks was one morning about dawn when I was observing. (Our lines at this place were only 45 yards apart.) Fritz evidently got my 'nut' in a good light and had a pot shot, the bullet passing across my face and knocking to smithereens the sandbag by my right ear. It partly deafened me for a bit – that's all. Seeing a couple of heads pass a gap one morning we commenced sniping and a Hun called out something which we could not understand. Then up went a white flag on a stick and it remained there all day. Evidently he wanted us to give away our position. We were not having any!

You said you wanted to know a few of my experiences, so I have tried to do so. But they are only the everyday experiences of most of us and are very tame compared to what thousands have gone through. Perhaps I will have something more thrilling to relate later on.

If you are picturing me writing this in a trench or dug-out, you guess wrong, for we are away from the scene of conflict for a couple of weeks spell – the half of which has already transpired. Our billets are situated in a picturesque locality, surrounded by hills and the trees are just bursting out into this summer green. After being in the trenches so long it seems a veritable paradise. We are practically isolated from towns and villages so there are very few temptations, if any, to assail the boys, and they are able to make the best of the spell. It took us 4 days to march here, and we will probably be expected to return in 2, so we shall need to be pretty fit. Today we have had a sports picnic and while I have been writing a football match has been in progress. The weather is delightful and all that is needed to make the day perfect are a few bonnie Australian girls to enjoy our picnic with us. (After the war, eh?)

It's a perfect evening for a game of tennis – how about it? By Jove, I would enjoy an hour or two on your court, knocking the balls about. Such talk brings back those happy days of the past; but I hope it won't be long before I am able to again challenge you to a game.

Do I remember the day Mag Badger and I were out mushrooming and we met you four and shared some biscuits? You bet I do! I remember vividly all those good times. I am glad Gladys and Jean haven't forgotten me; guess they will have grown out of all recognition when I get back for there seems to be a devil of a lot of Germans to wipe out yet.

We are going to have a concert this evening before we return to our billets. Won't you all come? These impromptu concerts of ours are worth hearing, I can tell you.

Now I must 'ring off' for the cooks have tea ready. Please give my kind remembrances to all friends and with love and best wishes to all.

I remain,

Your loving 'Coz'

Theo

Tuesday, May 29th 1917.
Left for L.G.S. at M.- [97]

Thursday, June 7th 1917
At 3.20 our big stunt – Taking of Messines Ridge.

<u>Somewhere in France</u>
June 10th, 1917
My dearest Homefolks,

I do not know now when the mail goes out or when the next one from home will arrive, so will write in any case, so that it should go before very long anyway. I told you in my last letter I believe that I had been detailed to attend a school. Well, here I am, and have been for ten days or so. I was sorry to leave the boys for I knew that during my absence one of the strongest of Fritz's positions would be stormed – and I would be out of it. Out of perhaps the greatest battle yet fought! The taking of this position is now a thing of the past and the Anzacs have added more laurels to their fame in the doing of it.

That was some days ago now and I have not yet been able to ascertain how our chaps fared, and more particularly how Bert and the boys in my team came through. I believe Bert is alright, but he is the only one of whom I have been able to learn anything. Naturally my thoughts have been with them all the time. Even tho' we are miles away from the battlefront, the thunder of the guns reaches us distinctly and they are seldom silent. Just now they are at it again – a continuous thundering rumble – but it is good to know that our boys have been able to take and hold the main objective, isn't it? I guess that 'ere this you will know as much and perhaps more than I of the taking of this particular position to which one I am referring.[98]

---

97 Messines

98 The taking of the Messines Ridge

I am pretty well acquainted with this particular sector in question, and can imagine the fight that must have occurred, even tho' I was not there. I guess it will be vastly different when I go back there, for such a bombardment would make it pretty well unrecognisable, I guess. Perhaps you will be picturing me taking a part, but instead I am away back behind the line trying to become more efficient in my work. However, if I have missed the recent stunt, perhaps I shall be better prepared for duty when I return to the line, after what I have learned here. Most of this course I have been thro' before, but other sections of it and also lectures which have been delivered are new.

We are kept well occupied during the day, but usually have two or three hours of the evening to ourselves which is mostly occupied in writing up the work done during the day and studying it. Best of all, we are able to have a good night's rest, which is an unusual luxury. I can tell you, 'tis great to be able to turn in knowing that no one will be calling you up to take a shift on watch, and that there is no fear of either Fritz himself or his shells making one tumble out when he has perhaps just turned in for a couple of hours sleep. Oh, know I am not indulging in a bit of a grumble just trying to draw a comparison of the luxury of sleeping on the hard floor of a barn or out on the grass in an adjacent field to what life is in the trenches.

Altho' I regret the necessity, I have never been sorry that I was able to come over and do my bit. But I am sorry that I had to come back here while the boys took part in the recent stunt. However, it won't be long before I am again with them, and I trust that my team still retains its good luck of the past and that they have come through alright, for we are staunch pals and have been together ever since we first joined up, almost; and I have been their corporal ever since we came over here, and we have always been on excellent terms with each other. I guess you will have received 'ere this the photo group of the team taken a while ago.

Since being at this school I have been into the town a couple of times with boys with whom I have chummed up. There are Tommies, New Zealanders and Australians from various units here going through the school and they are a fine lot of fellows without exception. Yesterday evening three of us, a New Zealander, a Queenslander and I, went into the town and had our photo taken together and we hope to get these during the week and of course I shall send one on as soon as I receive them.

It is very interesting listening to the experiences of such a varied gathering – men who have come from all parts, many have travelled extensively and a few have fought in others of the Empire's wars.

The New Zealander pal of mine comes from a station on the North Island and I like to get him talking about the life on the station. There are officers at this school as well as other ranks and one of them the other day told us some good yarns about his experiences with alligators and crocodiles up North and a sergeant told of how the natives in the Solomon Islands fight the sharks. Rather interesting, eh?

Now that I have told you something of my present doings and experiences, I will endeavour to reply to queries, etc. in your letters. Sure I do remember Millie's birthday and the happy time we had together. Quite a contrast to the way April of this year opened for me. (I told you in a previous letter how a patrol of Fritzs got into our line and down as far as my gun, but we sent them flying back!) I am very sorry that you have lost Miss Crittenden, knowing how much more work will be thrown on your shoulders Mother dear, and upon all of you, but trust that you will soon be able to get someone to take her place. Well done, Dad, how about cooking for us? I should like to have shared the meal you cooked.

I am so very sorry to hear about Roy Underwood. By Jove, I wish we had some of those superfluous pears over here, they would not be left to rot, I can tell you. The other night I paid 3 francs and 3d. for a tin of apricots (2/9). Some price, eh? (You see, Mother-mine, duty sent me back here instead of with the boys in the recent hard fighting!!)

No, Laurie, I did not fool anyone, but as you know a party of Fritzs nearly fooled me, but thank the Lord, they did not come off successfully. Do you know, a sergeant who was on watch at the time thought the one who told him about our 'little affair' was an attempt to fool <u>him</u>, and wouldn't believe it at first. Had he been with us he wouldn't have said anything about fooling. Millie got one home on Dad, alright, Ha, Ha! and she also had a good bit of fun at your expense; that <u>was</u> a good joke to put up. You described it jolly well in your letter and Bert and I had a good laugh, too. Fancy Ivey looking on my <u>old hat</u> with affectionate eyes – I wish I had been underneath it!

So Smut[99] has a great liking for your legs – you told that in a most original way, 'Young Un'. What a pity that you could not go to Gawler with Ivey, Mill; but I guess you had a good time with Mr. D. You don't tell me much about him; in fact, you seem to be very shy about that particular subject. You bet I remember your birthday of 1916. I say I should like to see you and Laurie walking up telegraph poles. How on earth did you manage it – did you stick on like flies. (You did not say whether the poles were in a vertical or horizontal position!) You must have been a lively crowd that night.

I must close this letter now as I intend writing a separate one to Dad. As usual I am in excellent health and spirits – <u>couldn't be better</u>. And I am so very glad to know that all is well with you all.

With very fondest love to each one of you and heaps of kisses, I will say *Au Revoir* for this time.
Yours Lovingly,
"Theo"

---

99 Smut – the family dog

Somewhere in France
June 17th 1917

My dear Dad,
My school finished yesterday and I am now on the way back
to rejoin my unit. We arrived at a rest camp last night and will
not leave until this evening sometime. My battalion is not far
away, for last night I met some of the boys from my old gun
team in an adjacent town and my word we were pleased to see
each other. They had such a lot to tell me about their doings
in the recent scrapping and made me more disappointed than
ever at having been sent back to the school. All the boys of my
team, with the exception of Bill Rettig escaped without any
hurt. Bill is missing. But Westley is O.K. too, I believe, altho'
I have not seen him yet.

With respect to the course of instruction through which I
have passed, I believe I pulled through the exam in good style.
For the written part of the exam. I received 95 points out of
100 and 'very good'; in the mechanical part I <u>think</u> I got the
same result. So I think a good report of my work will reach
my battalion course, altho' an advanced one, and I don't know
if the result will make any difference to me. So much for the
school!

By Jove, it can be hot over here as well as severely cold in
winter. I did not expect the heat to be very troublesome, but
I guess we have become acclimatised and feel it the same as
everyone else. Thank goodness we had a train ride yesterday
nearly all the way from the school to our present camp and oh,
it was O.K. It would have been killing going the distance 'per
boot' and with all our kit up!

So you are keeping in work – that is good! And work is
much easier when the weather is pleasant, isn't it?

Yes, Dad, our boys have been giving Fritz hell and I hope
to get to close quarters with 'em very soon. Over six months,

standing behind the sandbags, dodging the variety of stuff that he puts over, and with very little chance of getting one's own back, isn't much of a game. We all welcome the chance of pushing the devils back.

At our school there were New Zealanders and Tommies as well as Aussies and we had a great time together. We were specially drawn towards the Maori Islanders and I made many friends whom I was sorry to say goodbye to. The New Zealander in the accompanying P.C. was my special pal and we had some fun out of it. I nicknamed him Little Willie! We hope to knock against each other up the line before very long.

I will post these letters as soon as I get back to my unit, but I don't know when a mail departs. We are not told now, so have to chance it. I hope you will continue to receive my letters regularly, for I shall endeavour to keep my correspondence up to the mark. I'm hoping that a mail will be awaiting me when I get back to the unit.

I hope that your hopes and prayers will be speedily answered. Altho' we want to give the Huns, 'the father of a hiding' we are all, always thinking of home and loved ones and will be glad to get back again.

So *Au Revoir*, Dad, dear boy. I hope your health is keeping good and that there will be plenty of building to keep you occupied.
Ta! ta! lots of love from,
Yours Lovingly,
"Theo"

Sunday, June 17th 1917.
Returned from L.G.S. at M-

<u>Somewhere in France</u>

June 19th, 1917

My dearest Homefolks,

On once more joining my unit I found that an Aussie mail had just arrived, so I reckon I timed things nicely, don't you? Letters from you all were contained therein, so I was soon happily engaged in the eager perusal of them. That is the best day of all others – mail day!

Mother dear, Harry Cook <u>was</u> only slightly wounded at the time of which you spoke and was soon with us again; but the other boy was pretty badly hurt and has been in 'Blighty'[100] ever since, but is getting on pretty well, I believe. Archie Fletcher was slightly wounded after that but he got a 'Blighty' out of it and has had a jolly gay time. Archie will be with us again very soon, I believe.

We are glad that you are proud of us, Mother-mine, and hope that you may yet be still prouder. I think I understand how you dear ones must feel about it, but try and not be thinking too much about the hardships, etc., they are not so very great. At the least they are surmountable and we came over here to push the Germans back, and my comrades were very successful in that way very recently. I am only very sorry that I was out of the scrap. Still, I guess I shall receive my share before the job is finished.

You are an angel, Mother dear, to go to so much trouble to get those lovely parcels away to me and I cannot assure you too greatly how much pleasure I derive from them; and not only myself, but my comrades also. Fancy you going to all those

---

100 Getting a "Blighty" means being wounded and sent to England!

shops in order to get things for the soldier-boy's tin. Thanks so very, very much!

I guess it was a great help for you to have Millie and Laurie's help at Easter time. I do wish things were easier for you, Mother dear; but instead of you being able to rest a bit as the years go on you seem to have more to do. But you, too, are working in a good cause, and I am sure will meet with your reward. Give Auntie my love, won't you, please.

Re parcel, many thanks dear ones; it will be along in a day or two I guess. Parcels always arrive later than letters.

So Jack Warnecken is over here again. I must write to him. We may be quite close to each other and don't know it. Horace Billing is also somewhere about, but I have not run across him yet.

So Frank and Nell Ward paid you a visit. That's good; they are very great friends of mine you know. I have to go and see them when I return. Dear, oh me, what a lot of places I have promised to go to when I get back. It will be some job to keep the promises I think.

Well done 'Young Un', you will be beating Mill at walking soon, and she's a pretty good stepper. To hear that you are getting strong[101] enough to go the long walks which you did at Easter is excellent tidings. Keep it up, 'Young Un'! As usual, yours was a bonnie letter. Those sea things must have been pretty smelly for Mill to give you 3d. to throw 'em away.

At last, Mill, I have been given a little bit of information re a young gentleman named Daenke, who has evidently fallen a slave to your charms. And I don't blame him; it shows his good taste. The good times you had at Easter make me think of the happy times Ivey and I have enjoyed at the various places you mentioned. It was at Merino Rocks where I first made Ivey's acquaintance! You must have had a very busy week, helping

---

101 Laurel had appendicitis

Mother in the mornings and going out with your pal in the afternoons. No, I wasn't aware that May I. and Florrie K. are married. Is Bill Tink in camp?

Yes, Dad, our chaps are doing a bit of scrapping nowadays and Fritz is getting a very rough time. My battalion has taken part in a recent advance and did well. As you know, I was away at a school and missed it, worse luck. But now I am back with the boys again and hope to have a fair share in the fighting. You mustn't worry about me; I feel sure I shall come through alright; anyway I'm not afraid of the future, whatever is to happen. The boys have told me some thrilling stories of their experiences, and I felt very much out of it. The Huns seem to be getting frightened and that is a good omen, isn't it?

They are dirty fighters and after playing cowardly tricks on our fellows they whine for mercy – even get on their knees and plead 'Mercy, Kamerade'. Do they deserve it? No! And they don't get it either.

How is the poultry farm getting on? I am very glad to know that Ted and Daisy are getting along well – I never hear from them at all. If they do write, the letters never reach me. Is your block anywhere near where you, Fred, Ivey and I went for a walk just before I came away? Do you remember? You evidently have a jolly good vegetable garden, Dad; that's O.K. Your letters are always interesting, Dad, so write every mail, won't you?

I am going to endeavour to write separate letters to the other folk, so will say *Au Revoir* for the present. This letter may reach you at the same time as the last one which I wrote while at school, for I don't know when the mail leaves, you know.

So ta, ta! for the present, dear ones. Keep your pecker up. If a Frenchman wants to let you know he's feeling just the thing, he says *Tres bien*! That's how I am; *Tres bien*. So much for the present.

Fondest love to each and every one and heaps of kisses

From,
Yours Lovingly,
"Theo"

July 1917

Went in to occupy Messines Ridge Sector and was relieved on morning July 11th by another Australian B'de. During this period of 19 days, which was the longest stretch we have ever done in the trenches, our experiences were many and varied. For the first 5 days we were in the subsidiary lines, a distance of about 1400 yds from the Front Line. Our O.C. wanted me to dig a gun position and connect it up with the sub. line trench, so each night my gun team and I occupied about 5 hours at this job. The position commanded the La Douve River and as the German artillery kept the course of the river well swept with artillery fire we had any amount of projectiles bursting around us, the most annoying being the gas shells, the fumes of which caused us much discomfort; some of the boys being seized with dry retching, but they soon got over it. A night or two after our arrival it was pitch dark and we could scarcely see well enough to work in the early part of the night and to make matters worse the rain fairly turned down and continued 'till well on in the day. So we squatted on our heels with our waterproof sheets about us and made the best of a bad job. When day began to break we set about the excavating a place to build a shelter. When we had thrown up enough earth we visited one of the Fritz's old 'dumps' situated on the other side of the river, and secured sufficient material for roofing purposes and were thus able to make a pretty fair shelter, and as we are night workers over here we settled down to a good days sleep. After five days had passed we had to relieve the battalion who were in the Front Line. It was no joke moving over the open ground up to the Front Line, for shells had ploughed the ground up completely and old and new trenches, which had to be crossed and old barbed wire were continually hindering one's progress as we are always loaded up like pack mules. It was no joke. Twice on the way up I turned my foot slightly over but luckily no injury resulted. We arrived at our Front Line and walked along to our positions without once entering the trenches. It was better to stay in the open and risk a bullet or a shell instead of trying to get along narrow trenches with the load we carried. Our position was in advance of the Front Line in a shell hole, which post it was our duty to hold during the hours of darkness. On the first night I nearly shot one of our own officers and his batman. They appeared some little distance in front of us and seemed to be debating something. Having approached from the direction of Fritz's lines and appearing to be laying out some job, we of course took them for Germans. As I said before, I was on the point of firing when they turned and came towards us so I held my fire thinking it was going to be a soft capture for us. But I was disappointed, for, lo and behold, it was one of our new officers, a recent arrival, and his batman. When I told him how near he was to being shot he shook hands with us and said he was damned glad we didn't shoot. He had come from the support lines toward the Front Line, but the trenches were new and there were gaps at various points and he passed across one of these gaps to No Man's Land nearly to Fritz's lines. Luckily he became suspicious before it was too late and – you know the rest.

After spending a couple of nights in the previously mentioned shell hole we were removed to another advanced position on the left near the main road from Messines to Warnerton. We stayed here for a few days, our rations being brought to us during the night time. We were close enough to the German lines to see many Fritzs flitting about in the dark, hard at work apparently, but as ours was a post which we did not want him to know about we did not open up on such scattered parties.

However, I was itching to try my luck. So one morning I 'potted a Hun' who became very careless and showed himself fully. Just before dusk the same day I dropped another and that made them more careful in that particular spot. Heavy thunderstorms made the trenches like miniature rivers and our position almost unbearable, but not quite, and rations were short. On being relieved after a few days we took up our quarters in the support lines but it was a position, which Fritz shelled almost continuously, day and night. What with pieces of shell and concussion, and the blowing in of trenches it was a wonder that our casualties were not greater, and we had a few. But again my section was unharmed. One night I crept close up to Fritz's lines to observe for an officer who was going to take over a raiding party to clear out a strong point. It was exciting work, but I found the position was too strongly held for our little party. Next night a layer party tried to clean it but failed. The last 6 or 8 days we were back again in the subsidiary lines, where we had an easy job using our gun against the enemy aircraft.

Were relieved from Messines sectors about midnight and had a rough passage out over ground which was a network of shell holes over roads which had been ploughed up by our artillery in the big advance over Messines side. Fritz evidently knew the route for shells kept falling around us until we were not far away from our new billets. Here our brigade camped under canvas and for the first two days passed the time in eating, drinking and sleeping. After that we took up again more practice and instruction in our various methods of training. Several promotions have been made since we have been out, but so far mine has not come through, altho' I have on several occasions been given to understand that I would receive my Hind Stripe[102] when we came out of the trenches. Four days

---

102 Corporal

*or so ago my O.C. told me that he hoped to get another stripe
for me within the next few days. That's the last I have heard of
it. I have learnt by degrees that to become a 'specialist' one
throws away practically every chance of advancing, at any
rate higher that the rank of Corporal and it seems that it's a
case of a corporal I am and a corporal I shall be to the end of
the chapter!*

In the Trenches
<u>Somewhere in Belgium</u>
July 2nd, 1917

My dearest Mother,
Your last letter dated 29th of April reached me just after we came
into the trenches, about a fortnight ago. Thanks for telling me
about the flowers – I liked that – and how very lovely the rooms
must have looked with their masses of chrysanthemums. I can
picture them well, and in imagination I see you sitting there
writing to me. The thought just struck me – what a contrast to
my surroundings, a newly dug trench, where I am sitting in a
corner in the sun, pipe in mouth, writing pad on knee, writing a
love-letter to you, Mother-mine. Still, I'm comfortable and that
is one of the main things. Sometimes a shell bursts near by and
treats one to a shower of earth as one did a few minutes ago,
but that is all in the day's work and we have become quite used
to such minor details as that lately.

Yes, I can imagine you three on the early morning pilgrimage
to the window to gaze upon the wonders of the comet and your
description of it pushing itself into view over the tops of the
hills was a very vivid one. And I did hear that clatter too, when
the girls ran into the table in the dark!

Your wording of 'God Save our Womenfolk' is excellent
and voices our prayers. We trust that he will do so, for I look
forward longingly to the happy time when we shall join our

loved ones once more – Mother, Father, sisters, brothers and sweethearts. Jove, won't that be a time of rejoicing!

I was angry to read of the treatment that our womenfolk received on their march through the city. For one thing, I was pleased at the mark of respect that the gentlemen paid you. That was rather nice, wasn't it?

I try to follow your loving counsel and faith, Mother dear, as far as I am able. I try to play the game straight, so that I can have a clean record. Don't worry about me, Mother dear. I can say that I am not afraid over here and trust that a loving God will pardon my failings and if He wills it that I shall not return, then we shall meet in the Better Land. But, having escaped so far, I truly believe that I am destined to see this through and return to home and loved ones. Won't that be a joyous day!!

So, cheer-up, Mother-mine, I shall be returning one of these fine days and you shall be able to judge for yourself whether or not my experiences over this side have benefited me. They have – really! 'Tis said that experience teaches and perhaps no teacher could be so good as the life I am living.

'Tis hard to express these things, Mother dear, but I know that you will understand, and that the knowledge will make you happy. Actions speak louder than words and I trust that I shall be spared to return and give you proof positive and make some atonement for the many anxious times I have caused you. Oh, yes, I know I haven't been the boy I might have been – one has plenty of time and food for thought during the long night watches you know, and – I'm learning!

Now I must say, *Au Revoir*, Mother-mine.
Fondest love and kisses,
From,
Your Loving Son,
"Theo"

In the Trenches,
<u>Somewhere in Belgium</u>
July 10th, 1917

My dearest Homefolk,
I am still going strong in spite of Fritz's generous supply of shells, new trenches and a few thunderstorms thrown in. Taking everything into consideration, fighting in territory lately held by the Huns is much to be preferred to that of fighting in the old trenches for so long and having all sorts of missiles slung at us, without much chance of getting a bit of our own back. Now if Fritz gets very nasty the boys pay them a visit and endeavour to teach them a lesson, and generally meet with success. To show you the excellent spirit of our boys - one night German officers could be heard urging their men on to attack our line. Nothing transpired for a time, then the Huns only moved a little way from their trenches and started throwing bombs, and did not advance any further. Our chaps gave them a hot time and were calling out to them to 'come on!' That's the style, isn't it?

I still like the work as much as ever and my team is still favoured with a good share of luck. Out of the team whose photo I forwarded on to you some time ago, L/Cpl. Bill Rettig is the only one to 'stop one' and he got a trip to Blighty as a result of the recent big advance. I had a letter from him a couple of days ago and he is nearly alright and expects to be with us again very soon.

The other day I also heard from Horace Billing; he took part in the push and came through safely. Our units have been close to each other on several occasions but we haven't been lucky enough to meet yet. I may see him when we go out of the line this time, for I believe his crowd is somewhere in the vicinity.

A 'Burg pal, Frank Sharley, came to light with a letter from Egypt the other day, where he has seen fighting with one of the

Light Horse Regiments. He doesn't like it much over there; but I wonder which are the lesser evil, the sun and sand of Egypt or the cold and snow of France! France is not too bad in the summer but it's no good in the winter; so we are hoping the war will be over before winter sets in.

The Yanks are over here at last, Dad, to show us how to win the war. If they can finish it they are quite welcome to the honour!

Knowing that a number of boats fall victims to the submarines, it is almost certain that some of my letters fail to reach you. If sometimes there are big gaps between the letters, don't think that I have failed to write – I seem to be always writing and you should hear from me regularly. The fact that we don't know when an outgoing mail leaves may make a difference and letters may double bank occasionally; still I do my best and write often. I have already handed in a letter for yourself, Mother dear. You may receive it with this, or it may have been in time to catch an earlier mail. When opportunity offers I like to write to you all separately, but that is too big a contract to come at too often, so I usually have to make a general letter suffice.

You must not be disappointed not to know where I am and much about my doings, for the Censor would be certain to lay me by the heels if I touched on such subjects. Our letters, you know, are supposed to deal only with private and personal matters. The most important matter lately is that we are being 'fed like fighting cocks' as the saying goes, and it is a state of affairs which meets with our hearty approval, I can tell you.

I wonder if you received a couple of photos which I have sent you, the one of my gun team and the other of myself and two chaps with whom I chummed up at the school which I recently attended. I hope you have

Bert and I have for some time been going to have our photos

taken together, but so far that's as far as the matter has got. I suppose we will carry it out one of these days.

It is some time now since we have received a mail, anyway it seems a long time, and we are hoping to receive another one soon. I love getting letters, you all write so interestingly; Daisy and Ted are nice ones, though I can only remember receiving one letter from them since their marriage.

I say, Ron and Bert, my No.1 gunner, has a farm at Peake, which is not so very far from Geranium, and he says the latter town would not be at all a bad little place for you. By all accounts you could indulge in a bit of sport down there, Ron; so I hope you get the position and that it will only be a step towards a better one shortly.

In the big stunt our artillery was wonderful, absolutely combed the ground and knocked all the Germans' strong points to little bits. I have been over a part of the battlefield and judging by the attitudes of the enemy dead and the fact that they had flung away their equipment and that, many of the rifles were lying about and none had a bayonet affixed, the Fritz's must have been panic stricken. Poor devils!

I picked up a few German souvenirs on the battlefield, but subsequently lost them in a severe thunderstorm, which for a time made a mess of the trenches. Still, I guess there will be more opportunities later on of getting some. There are plenty of German helmets, rifles, gear and such like things lying about, but they are too bulky. It takes one all his time to get his own belongings about with him, without a load of souvenirs.

Those books which you sent me some time ago were greatly appreciated by us boys, Fred and Evelyn; and if any of you can send us one or two more we shall be greatly pleased to receive them.

I wrote to each one of you a week or two ago and will do so again as soon as time and circumstances permit.

Au Revoir for this time, with fondest love to each one of you and trusting that you are all in the best of health and that things are jogging along in good style.

Yours Lovingly.

"Theo"

Somewhere in Belgium
July 14th 1917

Dear Gladys,

In a letter, which I was pleased to receive from your mother a short time ago, she mentioned about your knitting me a pair of mittens and evidently you did not get my letter thanking you. The parcel reached me just after Xmas and as we were just on the point of going into the trenches I sent you a field card saying that I had received the parcel. When we came out of the trenches again I wrote a little letter of thanks. It may seem to you that I have been a long time before writing, but things have been happening over here and I have had not much time for letter writing. I like to receive your little notes, which you and Jean enclose in your Mother's and Dad's letters, so don't forget them, or I shall think you have forgotten me. We are fighting in the land where the little Belgian children used to live; they can't live here now because their homes have been all broken up by German shells and we only see children now and again in a few houses which don't happen to be knocked about so much as others.

With love to you and little Jean and Mother and Dad, I'll say 'Good-bye' from
Cousin
Theo

Tuesday July 24th 1917.
Received from LG Officer 48 pouches, mag. carrying and 24 braces.

<u>Somewhere in Belgium</u>
July 25th, 1917

My dearest Homefolk,
The last time I wrote to you was when we were in the trenches, and since then I have been living in hopes of receiving letters from home. But as we have learnt that mails have failed to arrive it is likely that we shall be some little time yet before we are once again happily engaged in perusing letters from home. I do hope that our outgoing mails have reached you safely, for I quite realise that the waiting of those at home for news is much worse than it is for us boys, especially when you read stirring news in the papers of advances that have been made. But don't you worry about me; I am in the best of health and spirits and am quite convinced that I shall come through alright. I'm beginning to think that my gun team is invulnerable for so far they have had quite a few bits of luck and that luck is sure to continue.

As we were in the trenches last time, (for a very long time in comparison to previous trips into the line) we earned a decent spell when our term was finished, and since then we have intermingled training with sport and have put in a pretty decent time. The weather has been delightful during most of the time, but we have had a few rainy days, and today is one of them. Our brigade is holding a sports gathering today and it's a great pity that it should be raining, more especially as previous days have been glorious. I want to do some writing before I go down to the sports ground.

Lately I have played cricket a few times and quite enjoyed myself and as a result of wearing a singlet my arms are pretty well sunburnt. You know I have never taken much interest in cricket, but have preferred tennis, football and basketball; still one takes advantage of anything that's doing over here.

On two occasions a party of us have walked to a hill from which we could get an excellent view of a part of the battlefront and you can guess how interesting it was for us. On Sunday the weather was just the thing and we visited this particular hill and witnessed a tidy little strafe of Fritz's lines by our artillery. It was a grand sight for us, but I bet it was no good to Fritz. During our wanderings we visited a farmhouse and refreshed ourselves with eggs, bread and butter, coffee and custard – how does that sound? I know that it tasted good!

Parties of entertainers visit us at intervals and treat us to an hour or two of good music and fun so you will see that we are having rather a good time; and the four battalion bands of our brigade provide us with plenty of music. Also our canteens keep pretty good stock of extras.

How is business, Dad, are you getting enough contracts to keep you going? I suppose your letter telling me of your visit to Dais and Ted has gone down to Davy Jones' Locker[103] along with the rest.

I hope that you have been able to obtain assistance in nursing Auntie, Mother dear, for I don't like to think of you doing so much. Give Auntie my love and I trust that she is keeping as well as can be expected, considering her age.

Are things going as well as ever at Sands and Mac's,[104] Mill? How are your studies progressing? Is Mr. D. still the favoured youth? You see I am asking a lot of questions because I have no news of your doings for quite a considerable time now.

I say, 'Young Un', how goes school; I suppose you are well up amongst the top grades now. By the way, I haven't heard any more about the pen painting, which you commenced quite

103 Davy Jones Locker – Bottom of the sea, the resting place of drowned seamen.

104 Sands and McDougall stationery store.

a long time ago. Have you been continuing with it? I s'pose you have grown some since I left and will be a second Millie when I return.

And you married ones, how are you all getting on and how are the kiddies? Give 'em all a kiss for me; I wouldn't mind being home to have a romp with them now; and to judge by previous romps I reckon we would have a lively time of it.

I wonder have you been transferred to Geranium yet Ron? In the last letters that I received it was thought probable that you would do so.

Are you still hanging on at Strath. Fred? Or have you been transferred to a more congenial post. Perhaps you are a P.M. yourself now and your own boss!

How are things going with you Gawler folk? Are you as busy as ever, George; and how are your eyes? How are the young 'uns, Con, is the new arrival behaving herself?

Dais, how do you like being a farmer's wife; and I guess Ted has found out long ago that it's quite true, too. I have not heard from you for ever so long and I suppose it would be just in keeping with things in general for you to have written and the letter was amongst one of the lost mails.

Haven't I asked an awful lot of questions, but you know that is only natural under the circs. I hope the mail boats will have an uninterrupted run in future and bring me piles of letters to make up for those that have gone down.

So *Au Revoir*, dearest Dad, Mother, brothers and sisters. Keep believing, for I shall be returning soon.
Fondest love to each and everyone,
from,
Yours Lovingly,
"Theo"

P.S. Is my insurance still holding good, please?

<u>Somewhere is Belgium</u>
Sunday July 29th, 1917

My Dear Friends of the Halfway House,
Letters from Aussie at last have reached us and included in my little lot were one each from Godmother and Phil, the reading of which I greatly enjoyed and was very pleased to learn that all are well.

If I remember rightly my last letter was written from the trenches when we were spending a specially long and trying time holding ground recently occupied by the Huns. We have had over a fortnight's spell since then, during which time we have combined sport with work. On most days the weather has been glorious and we have been able to have a good time, but there have been several short periods of very heavy rains and thunderstorms. At intervals parties of entertainers have visited us and favoured us with excellent programmes of music and humour to help brighten us up and make our short rest from the trenches extra pleasant. We have been hard at it since we came over here, and this rest is very refreshing and will put us in good fettle for the tough 'scrapping' that is to come.

While in the trenches last time the rumour that I had received several bullets in the stomach became current, and many of those who knew me were greatly surprised when my appearance assured them that it was incorrect. Another corporal of my company was wounded in that manner and died a few days later. A mistake somehow occurred that seemed to get my name in it; thank goodness it <u>wasn't</u> me! Bert W. did not go into the line last time with us and he heard the rumour and visited several dressing stations etc., to see if he could get any news of me. He was very pleased to find me just as well as ever.

I had several exciting experiences last time we were in, which I shall have to wait to tell you about when I return home. My Aussie mail isn't complete yet, for I have not received any letters from home, my married sisters' and brother's letters reached me alright, but none from Bakewell Road altho' Bert W. had one from Mill and Laurie, but I guess it will reach me in the next few days.

Our brigade held a sports meeting a few days ago and there was plenty of fun and friendly rivalry between the various battalions engaged. Some of our best athletes were not available, so our battalion did not put up such a good showing as usual, altho' we had a good many wins. The mule races for officers and men were the best fun of all. If a mule takes it into his head to go anywhere he will go – and nothing will stop him – as a result there were many extremely funny incidents. Some of the beasts were bits of outlaws and there were many falls in the attempts to mount them, but there was always someone who could master them. There were often bucking mules, bolting mules and jibbing mules all mixed up together, so you can see there was fun in plenty both for riders and onlookers.

The sports were well arranged and carried out, even to the extent of printed programmes. Some style, eh?

So, Vern Dunn is on the railway staff here! I haven't seen him since he arrived in England. I'm doubtful if I would know Reg Peake if I happened to run across him. I was shown the photo of girls who took part in a girls' frolic at the Mount, by a pal in the A.M.C. the other day, and I'm bothered if I could remember more than one or two! They were bonny letters I received from you and Phil, the other day Godmother, posted on the 29th May. I'm so glad the 'adopted sisters' and Millie are such good pals. I wonder if I shall ever meet Nurse Creasy. I would prefer the meeting not to be in the capacity of a patient, although no doubt it would be tip top to be looked after by such a nice girl!

It has been raining heavily nearly all day, so we have been confined to the camp, which perhaps is a good thing, for I have been able to do some letter writing. Our airmen, as they pass over the camp, are in the habit of giving us an exhibition of complete mastery of the machines; and they perform what seem to be the maddest tricks imaginable, turning, twisting, diving, falling over and over, doing a corkscrew descent and looping the loop, then, with a wave of the hand, swooping off at an incredible speed, probably to try conclusions with an enemy plane. Truly, they are wonderful fellows.

Don't forget, all of you that every mail I look for letters, and I enjoy <u>all</u> <u>very</u> much. 'Tis Sunday today and I would like to call in on my way back to camp as I did in the old days.

Au Revoir everyone!

With love and best wishes to all,

From,

Yours Sincerely,

"Theo"

Somewhere in Belgium

July 29th, 1917

My dearest Mother, Father, Sisters and Brother:

It is probable that we shall be engaged in some pretty stiff fighting very shortly and as Bert W. will not be going into the line this time I am taking the opportunity of writing a note to you all, which will be forwarded on to you, if it should happen that I am numbered amongst those who go under. Of course I am not expecting any such thing to happen, but I like to leave a note behind. I have never regretted joining up and I can truthfully say that I have enjoyed the life of a soldier. I have tried to play the game of life straight and clean and believe that I have succeeded.

The loving letters, which I have received from you all, have been very comforting. Believe me, your letters have been the best thing of all, and we always look forward longingly for

Australian mail and are never so happy as when we get letters from the dear homefolk.

Don't mourn for me. I shall be happy to give my life for the cause should the necessity arise. In writing home I have tried to give you an idea of my doings since I left Australia and I trust that those letters have been a small source of comfort to you and help you to follow me in my journeying to a certain extent, altho' the names of localities, etc had of course to be omitted.

If fate decrees that we are never again to meet in this life, there is comfort in the promise of a reunion in a far better land.

So with my dearest love to you all – Mother, Father, Bert and Ron, Con and George, Fred and Evelyn, Dais and Ted, Millie and Laurie, my nieces and nephews I say 'Good – bye'
Lovingly yours
"Theo"

Aftermath

69 Bakewell Rd.,
St. Peters
Thursday 2-8-17

Dear Theo.

I am anxious to get home today to see if there are any letters, and know how you are getting along. It's such a terrible time since we heard; 6 mails have gone out since one came in with letters from you. Last mail a few, not many, heard from France, and we were among the unlucky ones, we only heard from Mr. Warnie. The postman said another would be in today, so 2 must have come together.

Maud Mattner was down with us last weekend. She came down last Thursday, and stayed out at Wayville until Saturday. And then came to us until Monday. Of course Friday was Australia Day and town was <u>crowded</u>. There was a great procession, stalls along the streets, and different things on at the Town Hall and Exhibition, and there was a crowd <u>everywhere</u>. Sands closed soon after 11 a.m. for the day and so six of us went together. After the procession had passed we went to the Y.W.C.A. to dinner, and then down Rundle St., listening to the different concert parties, etc.

I went home before 3 p.m. and going down our road I had a buster. There by Opie's St. there was a lot of water in the gutter. I jumped over <u>as</u> <u>usual</u>, but – caught my toe and <u>down</u> I went, full length on the path, my parasol one way and I another. I must have looked funny I guess. I got up as soon as I was down, scraped my hands a bit and got my coat dirty. There was no one at home, I had Dad's key, so I did a bit of work and then cooked hot tea for the others. So they got a surprise when they came home. I didn't want to stay in town though.

Maud and I went down to Glenelg Saturday; there were such a lot of funny little things along the beach - squashy things, green balls, seaweed and stuff. The recent storms destroyed the breakwater and a little part of the jetty; it does seem a shame. We were home again before tea.

Sunday we went to Kent Town Kindergarten. (They want Maud to start one at Oakbank. They have a splendid one at Kent Town.) Afterwards we went out to Bert and Ron's to tea, and we <u>did</u> have a silly mad fit too. We were over at Opies' to tea Sunday week and didn't get home until after 11 p.m.

Daenke's have had no further news of the boys. I think I told you they had word to say Alley was seriously wounded. A few days after that they received two cables, one to say Alley had died of gunshot wounds in the chest and a fractured spine, the other to say Horace W. was suffering from gas poisoning. The same time they were handed the cables, they were handed letters from both boys, saying how well they were and had just received parcels. Isn't it hard? The young man, Mr. Smith, whom Miss Hunt was engaged to has been killed. Miss Marshall came around to see me a little while ago today; she got 2 letters from Horace Daenke. We had a letter from Dais and Ted at the beginning of the week.

Monday Aug 6th. 8.40 p.m.
Mother and Dad have gone to the Fisk Jubilee Singers; don't get a shock, it's so unusual isn't it. Laurel and I are alone, so we are writing. A mail closes Friday for letters only. I was trying to write yesterday but first the Marlow's came, then a boy, both to see father. Then Auntie Elsie and Violet Mather, and after they had gone came Ivey and she stayed to tea, so I got very little done. Mother went in to Pirie St. church Saturday night and she and Laurie to the Cathedral yesterday afternoon; there were special services. We went to Payneham to church last night. I am going out to Auntie Clare's next Saturday. They have asked me so many times and I'm going at last.

Poor Ivey is a bit worried and so are we. We didn't get any letters from you, not from you or Bert either. My word we did miss them too, but we can only wait and hope things are alright with you. I suppose the letters have gone astray; I wish they wouldn't though. We can't help wondering what is happening over there. I don't know when the next mail comes in. They say soon no boats there will be able to come out here, but I hope it doesn't come to that. It's bad enough now, it would be <u>ever</u> so much worse if there was no way of hearing at all.

Hugh Pala hasn't gone away yet; he is still in camp. Mother was talking to him Saturday. I had a letter from Marj Inkster today, you know Marj Agais rather. Her husband is in France; he is alright so far. She has a little boy, did you know? He is the best and most wonderful boy there is. That's what Marj says.

I'll leave off now, may write a little more before the mail closes. Goodnight.

<u>Friday</u> – No time for more so must go …Be good and take care of yourself.
Heaps Love and Kisses,
From Millie.

<u>Belgium</u>
6-8-17

Dear Mrs Wright,

It is with much regret that I write these few lines to confirm the death of your son, Theo.

I had been closely connected with Theo ever since we went into camp, and have been under him ever since he was made Corporal. His death was a great blow to me.

It was all our wishes if anything happened to any of us, that we would send a few lines home, and I am sorry to say I am the only one left of the Section to do it.

The only consolation I can convey to you is, that Theo died the death of a Good Soldier, and was loved, and is missed by all comrades and Officers.

Please accept my deepest sympathy with you in your great loss. Believe me to be ever,

Yours Sincerely,
No.306. Pte. C. Harding

<u>France</u>
8th August, '17

Dear Mr. Wright,
I thought perhaps you would like to know the circumstances under which your son came to his end.

Our Battalion with another had to take some enemy strong points and establish posts near his position. Your son in the capacity of Lewis Gun Corporal did splendid work until later on.

The day of 1st August he came to his death by an enemy

sniper's bullet. He nobly did his duty as a true Australian. We all loved him for his bravery and his capability in handling the gun he loved so well.

Will you accept of the deepest sympathy, which I offer on behalf of the whole of B. Coy.

I am,
Yours very sincerely
E. J. Colliver
Lt B. Coy.

Somewhere in France
August 9th 1917
Dear Millie,
I suppose long before you receive this letter, you will have received a notification from the Military Authorities telling you of poor Theo's death. 'Tis needless for me to say how I sympathize with you all, for my heart fairly bleeds for you.

Theo was killed in Belgium just over the borderline of France on July the 31st. On that day an advance was begun along the whole line, from here to the coast, and our battalion played a very prominent part in the advance.

Theo, along with many others went up into the trenches on the night of the 30th to take some enemy strong positions, but I did not have to go up there. So before Theo left, we shook hands and said goodbye, and Theo handed his pocket book containing his photos to me. Also he gave me two letters, one for Mother and one for Ivey, for me to pass on if the worst happened, and so I am forwarding on by this mail, the two letters and the pocket book.

The hop over the top of the trenches took place about 4 a.m. 31/7/17. All our objectives were taken, but poor Theo received a piece of shrapnel in the left leg, just by the knee whilst he was in 'No Man's Land', halfway between our own line and that of the enemy. He at once dropped to the ground, and one of his men stayed and bandaged his leg, helped him into a shell hole, and then had to leave him there, and go on with the rest of the gun team.

That was all the news that I could gather from the men when they returned first, from the trenches. These men when they came to be relieved in their newly won positions, did not happen to see Theo, and so gathered that he must have been taken away by the stretcher bearers. But as more men were wanted to go up to the trenches that same night to hold the trench against counter attacks, I asked the Colonel could I go up to the part of the trench where Theo and his team had attacked, and he gave me permission. That night I went up in charge of a gun team, and there, right where I stopped in the trench lay four men, dead. One officer - the officer in charge of Theo's party - and three other men; I didn't need to look twice to convince myself they were all dead, and 'Oh, my God', one of the men was Theo.

He had received a bullet wound right through the back of the head, but a smile was still on his lips and his hand still held his rifle. As this position where he was laying was further back towards our trenches than where one of his gunners left him in the shell hole, the only conclusion I can come to is that after he had recovered from the wound in his leg a little, he must have tried to crawl back to our trenches, and either a sniper's or machine gun bullet hit him in the head, for he was laying face downwards. Alongside of him lay two of his old gun team, Leslie Lovell and Tom Potticary. The shock I received I cannot explain, for I still expected to find him laying wounded in a shell hole.

On the 1st of August our chaplain and some stretcher-bearers came up to the trenches and carried the bodies away. Theo was buried just in front of our Front Line trench with two other men out of his team, Pte's. Potticary and Farmer. The chaplain's name is Huthuance. He conducted a short burial service over their grave. Two days after that I returned from the trenches to our camp.

Since then we have moved camp and are now back in France again. Theo once told me to tell you all, if anything ever happened to him, not to worry for him, because he had lived a good life and was certain that we should all meet again in God's own time. How much I miss him, God only knows. He was even more than a brother to me. And so the only consolation we can get, and the only message I can send, is that Theo lived the life of a Christian, and died the death of a true soldier. He was well liked by both officers and men, and is indeed sadly missed.

At present no cross marks the grave because it happens to be in 'No Man's Land', and if a cross was erected it would only be cut to pieces. But I would place one there myself if only permitted to. The military are going to erect crosses on all graves after we pass over the land.

So now dear friends, I must close.

From one who has lost a very dear friend,

Yours In Sympathy,

Bert W.

10/8/17

Dear Mrs Wright,

Enclosed is Theo's pocket book, which he entrusted to my care. I have already posted on the two letters, which he also left with me. One to you and one to Ivey. The quarter-master informs me that all personal effects Theo may have had in his equipment, as on his person, will be forwarded on to you in due course.

Yours In Sincerity,

Bert.

69 Bakewell Road
St Peters
Sunday, 19.8.17

Dear Cousins Nellie and Frank.
We have had bad news from the Military. Yesterday Rev.
Blacket came to tell us Theo died of wounds on 31st July. The
cable said previously reported wounded but we never received
word. Perhaps had we had word he was wounded we would
have been more prepared for this. It is terrible to get such word
and know we will never see our boy again. We don't know how
he was wounded at all as yet. It came as a great shock to us all,
it hardly seems possible for it to be true, though war is a cruel
thing. I can't write more, but we must let you know. You were
both so good to him and he thought a great deal of you all.
Yours sincerely
Millie

Jamestown
20th August, 1917

Dear Joe and Alice,
and family,
We had a note from Daisy this evening and we were very much
grieved to hear that dear Theo had died of wounds received in
action on July 31st. We all offer you our deepest sympathy in
your sad bereavement.

   We always had a warm place in our hearts for Theo. He was
always so bright and jolly and full of spirit. We trust you all
will have strength and comfort given you to bear up against
this great affliction, but you have the consolation of knowing
that he died for his King and country and for us, that we might
be free.

   His passing to the Better Land was 12 months all but a week

after our Alan, and now we have to endeavour to meet them over there later on, and none of us know how soon.

We know from experience what your feelings are, and truly sympathise with you in this great sorrow.

Yours very sincerely,

W. T. Palmer.

Jamestown
Aug. 20th, 1917

Dear Alice and Joe,

Oh I am sorry to know the sad news, about your dear boy. I have been wondering about him very often lately, but always hoped he would be spared to come home to you.

This war is such a cruel thing; I think I can see our dear boys, yours and ours, "Theo and Alan" as they were before you left the Mount. And now to know they cannot come back to us.

But we do know 'Our Father' has them in his care.

God bless and keep you all and give you strength to bear your loss.

With loving sympathy,

from,

Your loving Sister,

M. A. Palmer

Mount Gambier
August 21, 1917

Dear Millie,

Your letter and Laurel's came to me this morning, and their contents were a painful shock. I could not believe it at first, as there was, like with you, nothing to prepare me for the sad news. Mother, who had a very high opinion of Theo, joins me in sending heartfelt sympathy. Will you please convey this expression to all at home, as in writing you these few lines I am writing to all.

Even as you say you have thought Theo would come back again, so, too, have I. It always seemed to me that our friendship would be an enduring one, and that our future undertakings would be similar, and that we should be close together in our work. Theo was one of the few friends whom I regarded as 'my chum', and I am indeed grieved that our friendship has been so suddenly and cruelly ended.

I am afraid there is little I can say to comfort you. Losses such as yours seem so deep and poignant for human consolation, and our only solace seems to be to place our cross at the feet of Him whom we are told 'doth all things well'. In His farseeing wisdom He may have seen that it was the acceptable time to call Theo to Himself. I am sure all is well with Theo. Few know a boy better than his companions, and I can assure you Theo was a good, clean living youth with a deep love of home and the family circle, and a boy his sisters and parents might well be proud of. I am sure you all know this, but it is my opinion of my dear friend.

I am also grieved to hear Theo's young lady has lost her brother, as well as Theo. Though I do not know her, except through Theo, tell her I send my deepest sympathy as Theo's chum. I know how proud he was of her, and his high hopes for the future.

I must conclude now, Millie, with kindest regards to Mother and Father, and all at home, remaining, with deepest sympathy,
Yours Sincerely,
Frank Jaegar.[105]

---

105 Frank was a work colleague of Theo's from Mt Gambier.

STAR Office
Mount Gambier
Tuesday 21-8-17

Dear Millie,
I received your letter conveying the very sad news of poor Theo's death last night. It came as a great shock, more especially so as it is only a little while back since I had such a cheery letter from Theo. He used to write to me fairly regularly and I always passed the letters round to all the office staff to read. Theo was a general favourite with us all and it was hard to have to tell his fellow workmen this morning of the sad lot that had befallen him.

Please Millie convey my very deepest sympathy to your mother and father in their great loss.

My father is away in Brisbane at present, but I am writing him this afternoon. It will be a big shock to father, as no one thought more of Theo than Dad did. In the office and out of the office Theo's many sterling and manly qualities were always to the fore.

You mentioned Millie that you hadn't heard from Theo for three mails. Well my last letter was written on May 26/17. So if you haven't anything as late as that and would like to read my letter, I'd be only too glad to send it on to you.

Again expressing my very sincere sympathy,
I am,
Yrs. Sincerely
Millie Clark. [106]

---

[106] Daughter of Mr. Clarke proprietor of the *Star*

SOUTH-EASTERN STAR
Mount Gambier
August 21, 1917

Dear Mr. And Mrs. Wright and family,
It is with feelings of deepest regret that we heard of the sad and untimely death of your son and brother and our late comrade, Theo, and although we are fully aware that letters of sympathy are little consolation in such times as these, we felt that we could not let the occasion pass without conveying to you our sincerest regret.

Knowing Theo as we did, he was at all times a man in every sense. We feel his death keenly, and trust that the good life he led on this earth will help you to sustain yourselves in this sore trial.

He was held in the highest esteem by all members of the staff of the *Star* and died a hero's death, fighting for the cause of liberty and freedom. We trust that in your sorrow you will find some consolation in the promise of reward by his Maker as contained in the message, 'Greater love hath no man than this, that he laid down his life for his country'.

Again offering you our sincerest sympathy,
We remain, dear friends,
Yours sincerely,
Arthur R. Hill
W. H. Stanley
Millie Clark
J. Frimley
Edgar E. Chaston.

Pt. Wakefield
Aug. 30th 1917
To Mr & Mrs Wright & Family,

It is with deep sympathy that we write these few lines to you.

You may wonder who is writing but we have read with regret that your son Corp. Theo Wright died of wounds received on the 31st of July. Our poor boy Tom[107] was also killed on that day; we know that they were mates and belonged to the same Gun team.

So knowing the sorrow our loss has brought to us we sincerely ask you all to accept our heartfelt sympathy.
We remain,
Yours sincerely,
Mr. & Mrs. J. H. Potticary & Family.

If you should hear any particulars regarding their death we would be pleased if you would let us know.

---

107 Fellow soldier in the 43rd Battalion who died on the same day

PREMIER'S OFFICE
Adelaide,
South Australia
10th September, 1917

Dear Sir,

It has been reported to me that your son, Cpl. T. W. Wright, has died of wounds sustained whilst serving with the Australian Imperial Forces, and I desire, on behalf of the Government, to convey to you an expression of sympathy in your bereavement.

No one can render a greater service to his country than to give his life for it, and the heroic deeds of those who have fallen in the cause of liberty, justice and civilisation will be ever remembered.

Yours sincerely,

O. M. Peake

Premier

November 1917
The Officer in Charge
Base Records
Melbourne

Dear Sir
Will you please forward to me as soon as possible a certificate
of death of my son No. 937 Corporal Theodore Willard Wright
who was reported died of wounds on the 31st July last, while on
active service abroad; a member of the Machine Gun Section
of the 43rd Battalion Australian Imperial Forces.
Trusting you will oblige

Yours faithfully
Joseph Wright
Father of the above

Jean Park
Port Pirie
November 22nd, '17

Dear Mrs. Wright,
I am writing just a few lines to tell you that my Bert[108] has given his life for King and country. The Rev. Gowans brought the sad news to us Tuesday evening.

Our boy was killed in action on October 17 over a month ago now.

You, dear friend, will understand the sorrow that is in our home, the cloud seems very dark just now, and it is hard to see the light.

Yours with love,
Mary Westley

Port Pirie
January 10, 1918

My dear friend,
I am not going to keep you waiting so long this time. I don't know why I kept you waiting so long before. I suppose it was because time flies too quickly as a rule to get everything done that wants doing. But I often thought about you and wondered if all was well with you and your dear ones.

Poor little Laurie, she has indeed had a bad time. The summer is very trying when one is sick. I do hope 1918 will be a year of prosperity and peace and that the dear child will get well and strong and I hope Mrs. Hicks' little ones are better. I can quite understand how pleased they would be to see the little boy able

---

108 Bert Westley, fellow soldier in the 43rd Battalion.

to be at the table again. What a wonderful recovery. One can't wonder at the Dr. being pleased.

You only speak in your letters of one son. Is that the only one you have now? I remember you going to nurse him the morning we were coming home.

Fancy you having Christmas all on your own. I had all mine and yet I felt lonely and depressed. I don't know what kind of a day I would have had if most of our family were away. Lily and Stan are away just now on a long promised holiday to the home where I spent the early part of my life and from where I was married. It is a farm 3 miles from Georgetown. My parents are both dead and one of my brothers has the old home. Lily is well but very thin and frail. I hope she will be stronger when she returns home.

I am sending with this letter a memory card. Strange we both thought the same thing to put them together in a frame. I would like to ask you here if you got any of your boy's things back from the military such as his watch or any little keepsakes he might have had. Some Mothers get all their boy's things; others don't get any. Bert told me in the last letter I got that he was sending me a birthday card in case he would not get the chance later, but it has never turned up. My birthday was the 27th November. There is a mother living close to us. Her only son was killed 12 months ago and he was in Mitcham camp long after our boys left. He was with us in North Adelaide the last evening our boy was with us. She got a few of his things back long ago, but no one ever wrote to tell her anything about him. Poor Mother. I am so sorry for her. I have 4 boys left, but she has none.

I love reading your letters. You have great faith and it helps me to trust my Heavenly Father more. 1917 must have indeed tried your faith, but I am glad you look on the bright side and see the guiding hand of God through it all. Dear Mrs. Wright, what would our lives be worth if we did not trust and feel that all is well with our loved ones, and I hope this new year will bring us peace for which our dear boys died.

Look at all the soldiers that are coming back. I often think if it was best for Theo and Bert to come home, God would have spared them as well as the others. We make all sorts of plans but God alone knows if they will ever be carried out.

I think I will now close, hoping all is well with Mr. Wright, yourself and all your family. My husband seems to have grown old with the sorrow that has come to us.

From your loving friend,
M. Westley.

INFORMATION BUREAU
For Obtaining News of Sick, Wounded, or Missing Soldiers
SOUTH AUSTRALIAN DIVISION

Australian Red Cross Society,
Darling Buildings,
Franklin Street,
Adelaide,
20thApril,1918

Mrs. J. Wright,
69 Bakewell Road,
Evandale,
ST. PETERS

Dear Madam

No. 937 Corporal T. W. Wright. 43rd Battalion, M. G. S.

We are in receipt of a report by mail from our Commissioners concerning the above soldier, which has been gathered from Private W. B. Murray, No. 2526, from the same Battalion as your son. We would advise that as this report is only a statement of a fellow soldier, that it is purely unofficial.

Private Murray states that he saw the above soldier killed instantly, being hit in the head by a bullet. They were on an outpost in front of Warneton at the time, and Corporal Wright was buried by a pioneer party, where he died. There was no cross erected at the time. He further states that your son came from South Australia, and was a Compositor[109] in the civilian life.

Yours faithfully,
Chas. A. Edmunds.
Honorary Secretary

---

109 Typesetter for various printing firms

May 13th 1918
Major J. McLean
Officer in Charge
Base Records
Melbourne

Dear Sir

Enclosed, please find, receipt as asked for. The package was received about one month ago, but we have been hoping to receive also some important belongings of our dear son's. Such as, his watch, field glasses, a black enamelled tin box in which his presents were locked etc. Also I have been wanting to ask Miss I. M. Opie, the lady to whom Theo was engaged, whether she had received any parcel. As she had been ordered away by the Doctor on account of her health and I was called away to two different parts of the state, I have been unable to ask her, as when we did meet it was in public and therefore the subject could not be mentioned. Here I would like to thank the department on behalf of my husband – who is away from home, working in another part of the State – also members of our family, also myself for different articles and letters which have kindly been returned to us. Namely one tin, one pair socks, one chest protector, one diary. At different periods we have received those. And on last Saturday a packet containing cards, also two half pennies, which had been enclosed in a tin sent to the front for Sergeant B. Westley and C. Harding. I much appreciate the kindly act of those who had the handling of the tin. And as also I am glad that the rest of the contents were sent on to the comforts fund for distribution, as they would do more good thereby than being returned. And this mail, we received a packet of letters.

Please excuse mistakes in spelling, etc., It is so hard to concentrate one's thoughts.

Again thanking you

I am yours gratefully

Alice J. Wright

PS
We would like the authorities at the London B.O. to know how we appreciate their efforts. But as the typed address is not very discernable I cannot intimate them.

INFORMATION BUREAU
For Obtaining News of Sick, Wounded, or Missing Soldiers.
SOUTH AUSTRALIAN DIVISION

Australian Red Cross Society,
Darling Buildings,
Franklin Street,
Adelaide
1st August, 1918

Mrs. Joseph Wright
ST.PETERS

Dear Madam,
No. 937 Corporal T. W. Wright, 43rd Battalion
Our Red Cross Commissioners have forwarded to us a further report relative to the above soldier, same being supplied to them by No. 6410 Private H. E. Jarrad, of the 3rd Field Company Engineers.

This soldier advises that he did not see Corporal Wright wounded, but was in the same district at the time, and made enquiries about him, and was told by Private F. Tormay of the 43rd Battalion that while they were in the Front Line on July 31st, 1917, at Warneton, a shell dropped in the trench and wounded him badly. Your son died of his wounds and was buried at Warneton.

In his report Private Jarrad states:

"He worked for me at home, at Mount Gambier, and was the best mate you could want to have. He was a very good man in every way."

Our Commissioners have written to Private Tormay mentioned in the above report, and should they be able to obtain any further details, we will again communicate with you.

Yours faithfully,
Chas. A. Edmunds.
Honorary Secretary

INFORMATION BUREAU
For Obtaining News of Sick, Wounded, or Missing Soldiers
SOUTH AUSTRALIAN DIVISION
Australian Red Cross Society,
Darling Buildings,
Franklin Street,
Adelaide.

28th September, 1918
Mrs. J. Wright,
69 Bakewell Road,
Evandale,
ST. PETERS

Dear Madam
No. 937 Corporal T. W. Wright, 43rd Battalion, M. G. S.
In our previous letter to you we stated that our Commissioners had communicated with Private Tormay asking him for any particulars relative to the above soldier's death, and we are now in receipt of his reply, which is as follows.

Private Tormay advises that Corporal Wright met his death at the battle of Warneton near Messines, on the 31st July 1917. He could not supply any further particulars just then, but would later on communicate with our Commissioners after having gathered the necessary information. On receipt of his report we will forward contents to you.

In a report from Sergeant J. J. Mitchell, No.523, he states that on the 31st July our men attacked at Warneton, your son being in charge of his section. A shell came over and hit Corporal Wright on the leg and on his way back to the Dressing Station he was hit in the head by a sniper, which killed him instantly. Informant could not supply further particulars. Sergeant Mitchell further advises that Corporal Wright was of American parentage and worked at Mount Gambier, prior to enlistment, but his people lived at North Adelaide. Your son was an original battalion man, called Ted, but informant thought his name was Theodore.

Private T. Rooke, No. 971 intimates that Corporal Wright, who was a single man and lived at Mount Gambier before enlisting, was seen by him lying wounded in the open at Warneton when later on in the same night he was killed by a shot, being buried on the spot.

Should any later particulars come to hand we will again communicate with you their receipt.

Yours faithfully,
Chas. A. Edmunds
Honorary Secretary

<u>Renmark</u>
18 Dec. 1918

Dear Mrs. Wright,

I received your letter this morning and needless to say how glad we should be to get this dear letter, and how much it will be appreciated. When I think of the dreadful surroundings and horrors of war, and that those Brave Heroes find time to send a line to the home folks of a fallen mate. It is so good and kind of them.

Yes, James Allan Corney was my only boy and one of the best. He enlisted from the Adelaide High School in Dec. 1916, and went through the Signal School at Mitcham camp. He sailed with the 43rd Battalion on June 9 as Signaller to M. G. S. but went in the Machine Guns in England. He was killed on July 6 of 1917. His home name was Allan, but he mostly got Jim in Camp, and School.

I received letters from some of the lads, Private Will Algie was one who was with him when hit, also Alec Philpot and

Norman Lamming. He has since been killed, and I had a letter from Lieut. F. Osborn, his Officer, who sailed with them and returned sick just about that time. I have seen the account of his death just lately.

It was a hard blow to lose that Poor Lad, but my sorrows did not end there, for I lost my Husband on December 9th of the same year after four weeks severe illness. Why they should both be taken it is hard to understand for they were two of the noblest and best, after living happily together for 21 years. How hard and cruel is the parting. But I still have three girls who look to me for courage and strength so that I have been able to battle along for their sake. The oldest is nineteen years. and youngest nine. We settled in Renmark about the time the *Afric*[110] sailed. The people here have been very good and kind to us.

In the things returned there are a number of photos. I often look at them and would love to know who they are or something about them. Your Dear Lad may be amongst them. If you have a little photo of him would you kindly send one and I will return it again to you.

I will now close with kind thoughts and best wishes and thanking you kindly for writing,
I remain,
Yours sincerely,
Christina Corney.
Renmark
S.A.

---

110 The *Afric* was a 12,000 ton Battle ship that was sunk 13th February 1917 several months after Theo would have disembarked in France

Obituary in Mt Gambier *Star*

Corporal Theodore Willard Wright (Theo) (Ted) No.937. Battalion 43rd. A. I. F. (Machine Gun Section)

Obituary

Born December 30th, 1892.
Killed at Warnerton, Battle of Messines, July 31st August 1917.

He was born at Mt. Gambier, South Australia and was educated at Mount Gambier Public School, and at Mr. Carrozzi's Grammar School.

On leaving school he was apprenticed as Monoline Operator at the South Eastern *Star* printing and publishing office, Mt. Gambier. Owing to his father's breakdown in health, the family left Mt. Gambier and Theo was for about two years in the Petersburg *Times* Office. He was there when war was declared.

He offered for service but was rejected three times on account of defective teeth. This greatly troubled him, as physically he was splendidly fit and was anxious to 'do his bit'. As the Proprietor of the South Eastern *Star*, Mt. Gambier, had expressed a wish for him to return to the office, more than once, Theo did so. While there he had his teeth attended to and again offered for service and was accepted.

He entered into Camp on, or about, March 1st, 1916 and left for the Front on June 9th, 1916 on the *Afric*.

His indomitable courage and manliness was manifested in his eagerness to do his bit for his country, for after being rejected owing to defective teeth on several occasions he subsequently succeeded in passing the test. After being in Camp some time, his intelligence and general ability resulted in his being drafted into a Machine Gun Section. He showed marked proficiency and soon won promotion.

During his training on Salisbury Plains he was appointed Machine Gun Instructor and successfully trained a number of men in the use of these deadly weapons and was again promoted to rank of Corporal.

All through the severe winter in the trenches he kept fit and well and it is surmised that while serving with his Machine Gun Section at the front he received the wounds, which proved fatal.

On one occasion during last winter he, with his team, took part one night in a raid. They were up to their waists in mud and slush. Again he was recommended for promotion. When opportunity occurred he was sent to a school of instruction. But owing to disorganised service, the result has not yet been made known to his relatives.

Second Obituary

Mr & Mrs J. Wright of 69 Bakewell Road, Evandale, St. Peters have been notified that their son, Corporal Theo W. Wright, M. G. S. 43 Battalion has died of wounds somewhere in France on July 31. He was a native of Mount Gambier.

He served his time as a Printer on the Staff of the South Eastern *Star*, and about four years ago left with his parents. After a short stay at Oakbank he accepted a position on the staff of the Petersburg *Times* where he remained for two years, and then returned to his former position on the staff of the S. E. *Star* and from there he enlisted in January of last year.

He sailed for England on June 9th, 1916. After several months training at Salisbury Plains, sailed for France in November and remained with his Battalion until the end.

Some months ago he mentioned that he had been recommended for promotion and early in June he attended a military instruction school somewhere in France. He wrote to Miss Opie from the school enclosing a photo of two other students, one a New Zealander and the other a Queenslander and himself. He expected to rejoin his unit.

Newstead
27 Willams Avenue
Newstead
8th May 1929

To the Receiver of Public Money
Victoria Barracks
Melbourne

Dear Sir
The enclosed letter has just been received by me, and I am
enclosing a Postal note of six shillings for two commemorating
medallions of Menin Gate as per enclosed order form. I trust
these copies are still available, if not will you please return the
postal note.
am obliged
Yours Faithfully
Joseph Wright

Parliament House
Adelaide
19th November 1940

Mrs. J. Wright
27 Williams Avenue
Newstead

Dear Friend
I would like to extend my sincere sympathy to you in your
bereavement.
    Words seem difficult and futile but you will understand just
all I would like to say to comfort you at such a time.

It is always hard to part with our loved ones, no matter what the conditions, but remember that every black cloud has its silver lining, and so, we who are left, must just keep believing, and go on trying to make this old world better for the coming generations.

Again expressing my deepest sympathy and best wishes.

I remain,

Yours sincerely
Frank K. Nieass, M.P.[111]

---

[111] This letter was written on the death of Joseph Wright